Through Three Victorian Campaigns

Sir Charles A. Gordon, K.C.B., Surgeon-General

Through Three Victorian Campaigns

Experiences of a Regimental Surgeon
during the Gwalior War,
Campaigns in West Africa &
the Indian Mutiny

Charles Alexander Gordon, K.C.B.

LEONAUR

Through Three
Victorian Campaigns
Experiences of a Regimental Surgeon
during the Gwalior War,
Campaigns in West Africa &
the Indian Mutiny
by Charles Alexander Gordon, K.C.B.

First published under the titles
Recollections of Thirty-Nine Years in the Army

Leonaur is an imprint
of Oakpast Ltd

ISBN: 978-1-84677-768-4 (hardcover)
ISBN: 978-1-84677-767-7 (softcover)

http://www.leonaur.com

Publisher's Notes

Through Three Victorian Campaigns

Experiences of a Regimental Surgeon
during the Gwalior War,
Campaigns in West Africa &
the Indian Mutiny

Charles Alexander Gordon, K.C.B.

LEONAUR

Through Three
Victorian Campaigns
Experiences of a Regimental Surgeon
during the Gwalior War,
Campaigns in West Africa &
the Indian Mutiny
by Charles Alexander Gordon, K.C.B.

First published under the titles
Recollections of Thirty-Nine Years in the Army

Leonaur is an imprint
of Oakpast Ltd

Copyright in this form © 2009 Oakpast Ltd

ISBN: 978-1-84677-768-4 (hardcover)
ISBN: 978-1-84677-767-7 (softcover)

http://www.leonaur.com

Contents

The story of my life,
From year to year, the battles, sieges, fortunes
That I have passed.
—*Othello*, Act 1, Sc. 3

THIS PERSONAL NARRATIVE

IS INSCRIBED TO

MY WIFE AND OUR CHILDREN

CHAPTER 1

1841-1842. Gazetted to the Buffs
—Arrive in India

In 1841 British and Indian troops occupied Cabul; but throughout Afghanistan the aspect of things political was alarming. In Scinde the Ameers were defiant and hostile. The Punjab in a state of disturbance and convulsion; law and order had ceased; isolated murders and massacres instigated by opposing claimants to the throne left vacant in 1839, and since that time occupied by a prince against whom the insurrectionary movement was now directed by chiefs, some of whom were inimical to British interests.

Military reinforcements on a large scale were dispatched from England. Great, accordingly, the activity at Chatham, then the only depot whence recruits and young officers were sent to regiments serving in India. The depot then at Warley was for soldiers of the Honourable Company's service.

Into the General Hospital at Fort Pitt were received military invalids from India as from all other foreign stations. There they were treated for their several ailments; thence discharged to join their respective depots, or from the service on such pensions as they were deemed entitled to by length of service and regimental character. Then the period of engagement was for life, otherwise twenty-one years in the infantry, twenty-four in the mounted branches.

There young medical men nominated for appointment to the

army underwent a course of training, more or less long, according to individual circumstances, for the special duties before them; meanwhile they received no pay, wore no uniform; they dined at mess, paid mess subscriptions, and were subject to martial law.

Professional education included requirements for diplomas, and in addition, special subjects relating to military medicine, surgery, and management of troops. Nominations for appointments were given by old officers or other men whose social position was a guarantee in regard to character and fitness of their nominees for the position sought by them; certificates by professors and teachers under whom they studied were submitted to the responsible authority[1] at the War Office, with whom rested their selection. Thus in effect a combined system of patronage and competition was in force.

With anxious interest a small group of expectants awaited the arrival of the coach by which in those days afternoon letters and evening papers from the metropolis were conveyed. Eagerly was *The Gazette* scanned when, close upon the hour of midnight, the papers were delivered. Great was the pride and rejoicing with which some of our number read the announcement relating to them; great the disappointment of those who were not so included. The regiment to which I had the honour of being appointed was the 3rd, or "Buffs," the depot of which formed part of the Provisional Battalion then occupying Forton Barracks.[2]

The duties assigned to young medical officers were unimportant— initiatory rather than definite in kind. Careful watch and superintendence on the part of official seniors gave us an opportunity of learning various points relative to practice, as well as to ,routine and discipline, to be turned to account—or otherwise—in the career upon which we were entering. But the process of "breaking in" was not without its disagreeables. Courtesy towards young officers on the part of their seniors, military

1. Sir James McGrigor, Bart., Director-General.
2. The date of appointment as Assistant Surgeon, June 8, 1841. My diplomas—
L.R.C.S.E.; M.D. St. Andrews: both April, 1840.

or medical, was a quality rare at Chatham, but where met with in isolated instances was the more appreciated, and remembered in subsequent years. The "system "of training in force tended rather to break than bend the sapling.

Thus did three months pass away. Then came an order of readiness to embark with the detachment of recruits next to sail. Although about to proceed with those pertaining to what was now "my own regiment," official regulations required that my appointment to charge of them should have the authority of "The Honourable Court of Directors," and that to obtain it, personal application must be made at their old historical house in Leadenhall Street—a formality which was gone through with ease and success. This is what the appointment in question implied:—Not only did I receive the free passage to which I was entitled, my daily rate of pay [3] running on the while, minus £5 deducted "for messing," but was privileged to occupy the second best cabin on board, and at the end of the voyage to receive in *rupees* a sum equivalent to fifteen shillings per head for officers and soldiers landed, and half a guinea for each woman and child. In those "golden days" the sterling value of the *rupee* was at *par*.

The ordeal of "inspection" was duly performed, the requirements on board declared "satisfactory," the formal report to that effect transmitted to the authorities. My personal knowledge of those requirements was absolutely nil. How much more definite that of other members of the Inspecting Committee, was soon to be judged of. For example: side or stern ports there were none, deck ventilators being considered sufficient. Food stores comprised casks of salted beef and pork; tins of soup and *bouillé*, potatoes and other vegetables, some dried, some tinned; pickles and lime juice, bread, otherwise hard biscuit, destined ere many weeks had elapsed to become mouldy and honeycombed by weevils. There were bags of flour, peas, and raisins; an ample supply of tobacco; also of rum and porter, to be issued to the troops as a daily ration.

The water tanks and a series of casks on deck had been

---

3. 7s. 6d.

filled—so it was said—from the Thames below London Bridge, when the tide was at its lowest.

The day of departure arrived. The detachment of which I was an unit marched away from Chatham Barracks, through Rochester, Strood, and so by road to Gravesend. There it was conveyed on board the *Indian;* twenty-four hours allowed us to settle down on board; the ship then taken in tow by steamer; we are on our voyage.

A fortnight elapsed; we were no farther on our way than off the coast of Spain. The novelties of first experience afforded subject of observation and thought: those which most impressed us, the clear moonlight, the starry galaxy of the heavens, the Milky Way, the cloudless sky, the phosphorescence of the undulating sea through which our ship slowly glided; the masses of living things, chiefly *medusæ*, that floated fathoms deep in ocean. During daylight many land birds flew over us or rested on the rigging.

Small though our party was, it comprised its proportion of men typical in their several ways. The commander of the vessel, soured with life, disappointed in career, tired of sea life, but unable to quit his profession. One of the ship's officers, a young man of deeply religious convictions. An ancient subaltern, inured to the chagrin of having been several times purchased over by men of less service but more fortunate than himself in worldly means. The lady's man, pretentious and vapid, given to solos on a guitar; the instrument adorned with many coloured ribbons, to each of which he attached a legend; his cabin decorated with little bits of "work," cards, and trinkets, for as yet photographs had not been invented. The irascible person, ready to take offence at trifles, and in other ways uncertain.

A month on board; the Canary Islands faintly seen in the distance. Already heat and stuffiness 'tween decks so unpleasant that carpenters were set to work to cut out stern ports for ventilation. Our progress so slow that with all sails set a ship's boat was launched, in which some of our numbers amused themselves by rowing round the vessel.

Two months, and we still north of the Equator. Various reasons given for tedious progress, among others light airs, contrary winds, adverse currents. But none of these explained the fact of our being passed by vessels, some of which, on the horizon astern of us in the morning, were hull down on that ahead ere daylight vanished. That our ship was alluded to as "a worthless old tub" need now be no matter of surprise.

Not more than one-third of our distance to be run as yet got over; prospects as regarded the remainder by no means happy. The unwelcome announcement made that all hands, including crew and troops, must submit to reduced allowance of food and water. Of the latter, the full allowance per head per day for cooking and all other purposes was seven pints, now to be reduced to six. No wonder that the announcement was not received with tokens of approval.

Looking back to conditions as described in notes taken at the time, the contrast so presented between those .which were then deemed sufficient for troops on board ship, and those which now exist may not be without some historical interest. Space 'tween decks so limited,[4] that with men's hammocks slung, those who on duty had to make their way along at night were forced to stoop almost to the attitude of the ordinary quadruped. The "sick bay" on the port side, close to the main hatch, directly exposed to rain from starboard; except a canvas screen, no separation between the quarters of unmarried and those of married; no separate accommodation for sick women or children; no prison set apart for the refractory. All over the ship myriads of cockroaches; these insects, especially lively at night, supplied to men and officers excitement and exercise, as, slipper in hand, they hunted them whenever the pale light given by the ship's lamps enabled them to do so.

Cleanliness of decks and fittings was to some extent effected by means of dry scrubbing. The use of Burnett's Solution [5] substituted the odour of the compound so named for that of humanity. By means of iron fumigators in which was burning tar,

---

4. The hammock space per man was 9 feet x 1½.
5. Solution of chloride of zinc..

the atmosphere of 'tween decks was purified, due precautions taken to minimise the risks of fire attending the process. Tubs and hose on deck supplied ample means for the morning "souse."

A carefully chosen library provided for the use of our men was placed on board by the Indian authorities; it was highly appreciated and generally made use of. Among the troops, games of all sorts were encouraged, their selection left to men's own choice. In working the ship ready hands were at all times available. Gymnastics and feats of strength were in high favour, and so, with the routine of guards, parades, inspections, and so forth, daytime was filled up. In the evenings, songs, recitations, theatrical performances, and instrumental music were indulged till the bugle sounded "lights out."

Officers had their ways of passing the time. They included games, gymnastics, bets, practical jokes (of all degrees of silliness), cock fighting, wild and dangerous adventures in the rigging, and on Saturday evenings, toasts, then usual on such occasions, enthusiastically "honoured." A weekly newspaper was set on foot; the works of Scott, Shakespeare, and Pope, among other authors, carefully studied, and discussions, more or less profitable, held on their contents.

Sighting, signalling, and hailing ships was a favourite amusement as opportunity occurred. By some of those homeward bound we dispatched letters, with passengers on board others we exchanged visits, strange as such ceremonies may seem to those now acquainted only with modern twenty-knot floating steam palaces. While paying such a visit to a ship five months out from China, we learned the "news" that Canton had been captured (on May 25-27, 1841) by the forces under command of Sir Hugh Gough.

In near proximity to the Equator we came upon a ship, the *Cambridge*, disabled, her topmasts carried away in a sudden squall two nights previous. The resolve to stand by and give assistance was quickly taken. Boats were lowered, parties of sailors and recruits, accompanied by some officers, were soon on board. Within a few hours defects were made good as far as that was practicable;

meantime night had closed in, a somewhat fresh breeze sprung up, clouds obscured the sky, and so the return to our ship was by no means accomplished without danger.

The distance to be got over was still great before the ship could reach Table Bay and renewed supplies obtained. The health of all on board had so far remained good, notwithstanding all the drawbacks experienced. The likelihood, however, that this happy state of things might suddenly come to an end became to me a source of what was the first sense of official anxiety with which I had been acquainted.

Excepting two somewhat elderly non-commissioned officers, specially put on board the better to ensure discipline among our recruits, all others were as yet but partly tutored in military duties and order. Unwilling obedience had from the first been shown by several of their number; then came irregularities, quarrels, and fights among themselves. Nor were the few married women on board ideal patterns of gentleness, either in speech or behaviour.

Among the crew were men whose antecedents, so far as they could be ascertained, were of the most questionable kind, and whose conduct on board had, from the first, been suspicious. Between them and kindred spirits among the recruits, it appeared that an understanding had been come to to have what they called "a disturbance" on board. Those intentions having come to the ears of the officers, with the further information that fully ninety men were implicated, preparations were made for emergencies: arm-racks fitted up in the saloon; fire-arms burnished; ammunition seen to; non-commissioned officers instructed as to their duties. But an occurrence which now happened distracted attention from the so-called plot, whether real or imaginary did not transpire.

Our entrance into tropical latitudes, some three weeks previous, had been duly announced by "Neptune," who, selecting the period of first night watch for the ceremony, welcomed us from amidst a flare of blue lights on the forecastle, on our coming to his dominions. Having done so, he returned to his element;

his car a burning tar-barrel, which we continued to watch as it seemed to float astern, until all was darkness again. On board, "offerings" had to be made to the sea-god, half-sovereigns and bottles of rum, sent to the fo'c's'le, being those most appreciated.

While yet in the first degree of south latitude, the sea-god, accompanied by his court officials, announced their arrival on board, the whole personified by members of the ship's crew, appropriately attired in accordance with their respective official positions. The ceremony of "initiating" the "children" was quickly in progress, the chief ceremonies connected therewith including shaving, "bathing," besides some others by no means pleasant to their subjects. One of our young recruits strongly resisted the ordeal through which several of his comrades had passed. He succeeded in making his escape from his captors, and quickly mounting the ship's railing, thence plunged into the sea, to the consternation and horror of us all. The vessel was instantly "put about," a boat lowered, but search for him was in vain. The occurrence was, indeed, a melancholy outcome of what was intended to be a scene of amusement. But the spirits of young men were light, and ere many hours had elapsed, the song and dance were in progress, as if the event had not occurred. A Court of Inquiry followed in due time, and then the incident was forgotten.

We were now approaching Table Bay. Great was the interest and admiration with which we looked upon Table Mountain, as its grandeur became more and more distinctly revealed. Hardly less was our estimate of the Blue Berg range, by which the distant view was bounded. Soon we were among the shipping, and at anchor.

Our ship was soon surrounded by boats, that seemed to come in shoals from shore; some conveying fruit and curiosities for sale, others suspected of carrying commodities less innocuous in kind. But sentries, already placed at gangways and other points on deck, prevented traffic between our men and the small craft. The aspect of boats and their crews was alike new and strange to most of us: the former, striped with gaudy colours, red, black, and white; the latter, representing several nationalities, including

English, Dutch, Malay, East Indian, and typical African, their several styles of costume no less various than themselves.

Some of our number, proceeding ashore, stood for the first time on foreign ground. Cape Town presented a series of wide, regularly arranged streets, intersecting each other, their sides sheltered by foliage trees. Flat-roofed houses, coated with white plaster, were nearly invariable in their uniformity. Great wagons, drawn by teams of oxen, from six to twelve in number—and even more—were being driven along by Malays, armed with whips of alarming proportions; though, fortunately for the beasts of burthen, they were little used. Crowds of pedestrians were on the thoroughfares, interspersed with guardians of the peace, the latter dressed after the manner of their kind in London. It was the month of December; but the temperature was that of summer; the heat oppressive, as we continued our excursion.

Part of that excursion was to Constantia. On the right, the great mountain, rising to a height of three thousand feet; the space between its base and the road along which we drove thickly covered by forest and undergrowth, the whole comprising oaks, silver and other pines, geraniums, pomegranates, and heaths, interspersed with herbaceous plants bearing gorgeously coloured flowers. At intervals there were richly cultivated fields and valleys; on or near them attractive-looking houses, many having attached to the latter no less handsome gardens. The road was thickly occupied by vehicles and pedestrians; among the whites, a considerable proportion of well-looking individuals of the fair sex. There was, in fact, a general aspect of activity and of prosperity.

The ordeal of "reporting ourselves" to the authorities was gone through: our reception by one, whose surname indicated Dutch origin, ungracious and supercilious; by the departmental chief so kindly, as by contrast to make an impression upon us, but partially inured to official ways as we then were. Meanwhile, the necessary steps were in progress for placing on board our ship the much-needed supplies of food materials and of water.

Among vessels that anchored in the bay during our detention, there was the ship *Lloyds,* having on board emigrants from England to New Zealand. When first they began their voyage, they numbered eighty women and 117 children; but so appalling had been the mortality among them that, of the children, fifty-seven had died. In all parts of the space occupied by passengers, sickness and distress in various shapes prevailed. Children, apparently near to death, lay in cots by the side of their prostrate mothers, whose feebleness rendered them unable to give the necessary aid to their infants.

A state of indescribable filth existed everywhere; ventilation there was none in the proper sense. Women and children affected with measles in very severe form, that disease having been brought on board in the persons of some of those embarking; others suffered from low fever, and some from scurvy, which had recently appeared among them. The family of the medical man on board had suffered like the others, one of his children having died. On the deck of the ship lay two coffins, containing bodies of the dead, preparatory to being taken on shore for burial. The entire scene presented by the ship, the saddest with which, so far, I had become acquainted.

In Table Bay we again met the *Cambridge* already mentioned, that vessel arriving shortly after our own had anchored. In a sense we, the passengers of both, greeted each other as old friends; visits were interchanged, then leave was taken of each other with expressions of good wishes. By-and-by there came to anchor the ship *Nanking,* having on board recruits belonging to the service of the Honourable Company. Greetings and cheers were interchanged; for were we not all alike proceeding on a career, hopeful indeed, but as yet uncertain?

In the castle, a short distance from Cape Town, the 25th Regiment, or Borderers, was stationed, and in accordance with the hospitable custom of the time, an invitation to dinner with the officers was received on board. The party on that festive occasion numbered seventy, the majority guests like ourselves, and now the circumstance is mentioned as showing the scale upon which such entertainments were given.

Invited to the house of an Afrikander Dutchman,[6] we found ourselves in large airy rooms, destitute of carpets, with polished floors; wall space reduced to a series of intervals between doors and windows; the arrangements new to us, but suited to climatic conditions of the place. Little attentions shown by, added to personal attractions of, lady members of the family naturally enough left their impression on young susceptibilities.

Very interesting also, though in a different way, was our visit to the house of Baron von Ludovigberg. Elegantly furnished, rooms so arranged as to be readily transformed into one large hall, everything in and around marking a life of ease and comfort. His garden, situated in Kolf Street, extensive, elegantly laid out, with large collection of plants indigenous and foreign; at intervals fountains and ornamental lakes. In the latter were thousands of gold fish, so. tame as to approach and feed from the hand of an attendant; to the sound of a handbell rung by him they crowded, though on seeing us they kept at a distance. To the sound of the same bell when rung by us they would approach, but not come near the strangers.

Our voyage resumed, away eastward we sailed. Sixteen days without noteworthy incident; then sighted the island of Amsterdam, from which point, as the captain expressed it, he began to make his northing.

Another interval of monotonous sea life. At daybreak we found that in close proximity to us was a barque, the *Vanguard,* on board of which there was disturbance amounting to mutiny among the crew. The captain[7] signalled for assistance. A party of our young soldiers, under command of an officer, proceeded on board, removed the recalcitrant men to our ship, some of our sailors taking their place, and so both vessels continued their way to Calcutta.

Again was the unwelcome announcement made that short allowance of food and water was imminent, to be averted by progress of our vessel becoming more rapid than it had hitherto

---

6. Mr. Mechi.
7. Captain Gurwood.

19

been. The tedium of the voyage had told upon us; idleness had produced its usual effect chafing against authority and slow decay of active good fellowship became too apparent; all were tired of each other.

Another interval. From the mast-head comes the welcome sound, "Land on the starboard bow." Soon we come in view of low-lying shore, over which hangs a haze in which outlines of objects are indistinct. What is seen, however, indicates that our ship is out of reckoning; that, as for some time past suspected, something has gone wrong with the chronometers. Wisely, the captain determines to proceed no farther for the present, until able to determine our precise position. A day and night pass, then is descried a ship in the distance westward. We proceed in that direction, and ere many hours are over exchange signals with a pilot brig.

Twenty-four weeks had elapsed since the pilot left us in the Downs; now the corresponding functionary boards our ship off the Sand-heads. We are eager for news. He has much to tell, but of a nature sad as unexpected. The envoy at Cabul, Sir William Macnaughten, murdered by the hand of Akbar Khan; the 44th Regiment annihilated, part of a force comprising 4,500 fighting men and 12,000 camp-followers who had started on their disastrous retreat from Cabul towards the Khyber Pass; one only survivor, Dr. Bryden, who carried tidings of the disaster to Jellalabad. Another item was that several officers, ladies, and children were in the hands of the Affghan chief.

Progress against the current of Hooghly River was slow, steam employed only while crossing the dreaded "James and Mary" shoal; for then tugs were scarce, their use expensive. Three days so passed; the first experience of tropical scenery pleasant to the eye, furnishing at the same time ample subject for remark and talk. On either side jungle, cultivated plots of ground, palms, bamboos, buffaloes and cattle of other kinds. In slimy ooze gigantic gavials; in the river dead bodies of animals and human beings, vultures and crows perched upon and tearing their decomposing flesh. Native boats come alongside; their swarthy, semi-naked crews scream and gesticulate wildly as they offer for sale fruit and other commodities. Our rigging is crowded with *brahminee* kites and other birds; gulls and terns swarm around. The prevailing damp heat is oppressive. Now the beautiful suburb of Garden Reach is on our right; on our left the Botanic Garden; the City of Palaces is ahead of us; we are at anchor off Princep's Ghat.

The "details," as in official language our troops collectively are called, were transferred to country boats of uncouth look, and so conveyed to Chinsurah, then a depot for newly arrived recruits. Our actual numbers so transferred equalled those originally embarked, two lives lost during our voyage being made up for by two births on board. Sanitation, in modern significance of the term, had as substitute the arrangements—or want of them—already mentioned; yet no special illness occurred; my first charge ended satisfactorily.

CHAPTER 2

1842-1843. In Progress to Join

First impressions of this our first station in India, recorded at the time, were:—

Houses of mud, roofs consisting of reeds, fronts open from end to end; members of families within squatting, infants sprawling, in a state of nudity, upon earthen floors made smooth and polished by means of cow-dung applied in a liquid state; while to outside walls cakes of the same material are in process of drying, to be thereafter used as fuel by Hindoos. Gardens and cultivated fields abound; flowering trees and shrubs, cocoa palms, banana bushes, clumps of bamboo, rise above dense undergrowth of succulent plants.

A heavy, oppressive atmosphere, pervaded by odours, sweet and otherwise, has a depressing effect, as if conditions were not altogether wholesome. European houses according to Holland model, terraces and gardens giving to them an attractive and elegant appearance, indicating the importance of the place while in the hands of the Dutch, prior to date [1] of the treaty in accordance with which it was by them exchanged for Java. An extensive range of spacious barracks and supplementary buildings added much to the beauty of the station.

Before many days were over several of our young lads had fallen victims to cholera. In this our first experience of that disease we had access to no one capable of giving aid and advice; we were left to individual judgment, and it altogether astray as

1. 1815

to the appropriate method in our emergency. For a time, out of our small party death claimed several daily victims; young wives were thus left widows, young children orphans.

Glad to receive orders of readiness to resume progress by river to next stage of our journey. Then arrived two senior officers,—one to take military command;[2] the other, departmental charge of our detachment. Country boats provided as before, others of better kind for officers. Our unwieldy fleet started at the appointed time;[3] the boats comprising it straggled irregularly across the river, and having gained the opposite bank, there made fast for the night.

Early next morning it was in movement. Midday heat became oppressive. One of the soldiers was prostrated by cholera, another by sun fever. Inquiry revealed the unpleasant fact that the "experienced" officer recently appointed for the purpose had made no arrangements whatever for sick. Those fallen ill were now sent in small boats back towards Chinsurah; and so we continued our river progress, steps being taken to have deficient requirements sent on without delay.

Next evening was far advanced ere they arrived. The numbers of our sick had increased, several deaths taken place, some with appalling rapidity in the absence of means of help. The great heat prevailing made early interment necessary. Graves had to be hastily made in groves of trees near the river bank; to them the dead were committed, our fleet continuing its progress, sailing or tracking[4] according to wind and current. After night had fallen, the blaze of funeral pyres on the river banks told their tale of pestilence.

For several days mortality was great in our small party, and among the native boatmen. As deaths occurred among the latter, the bodies were simply left on the bank to be devoured by jackals, dogs, and vultures, numbers of which were in wait for prey. Some of our boats sprung leaks, and so became useless; nor was

---

2. Captain Astier, 62nd Regiment.
3. March 28, 1842.
4. *i.e.,* drawn by means of ropes attached to their masts.

it an easy matter to get them replaced. Men and stores had to be got out as best they could and disposed of among others—proceedings by no means easy under then present circumstances.

At last there came an interval in which the malign influence of our invisible enemy seemed as if withheld. While gliding upwards against the silent river current, suddenly from one of the men's boats there burst a mass of thick smoke, speedily followed by flame, and within the space of a few minutes nothing except the charred framework remained. How, or by what means, the occupants of the boat escaped did not transpire; that they did so was fortunate for themselves and satisfactory to all, though the accident, subsequently ascertained to have resulted from their own carelessness, destroyed their entire kits and other belongings.

Short was our respite. Suddenly and fatally was our detachment again struck, several deaths by cholera occurring in quick succession. Our somewhat eventful "voyage" was near its end, when in midstream two of our boats came violently in collision with each other, considerable mutual damage being the result. An unfortunate panic occurred among the recruits on board, one of whom leapt overboard and so disappeared. Soon afterwards our journey was at an end, it having occupied eleven days; we arrived at Berhampore.

Near to the spacious range of barracks in which our young soldiers were accommodated were lines occupied by a native regiment, (21st)—at that time reputed to be of distinguished loyalty to Jan Kompanee, with whose liberal dealings towards its own proper servants all were so well pleased. In others were invalids, soldiers' wives and children pertaining to regiments (Namely, 26th, 49th, and 55th) employed in the war proceeding against China; many as yet unaware that they had been made widows and orphans by the climate of Chusan and coast generally.

Here the conduct of our lads—for they had scarcely become men—became so reckless that military discipline had to be rigidly enforced, while in many instances severe or fatal illness seemed to be the direct result of their own misconduct. As a ready, and as thought at the time effectual, means of coercion, corporal punishment was awarded by courts-martial. The ordeal of being present during its infliction was nauseating; but constituted as the detachment was, the punishment seemed to have been in all cases well deserved.

General Raper was the officer in political charge of the *Nawab* of Moorshedabad, then a boy of some ten years old. Several civilians high in rank, and a few non-official residents, for the most part connected with the manufacture of *tussar*[5] silk, resided at Berhampore. From several of them we young officers received much attention and kindness, not only in their own houses but on excursions organized by them for our special benefit. Prominent among those who thus befriended us, young "griffs" as we were, General Raper and Charles Du Pre Russell are remembered gratefully—even while these notes are penned, many years after the date and incidents referred to.

In due time the order arrived for us to resume our river journey, our destination Cawnpore; again country-made boats our means of transport. In the early days of August we started on what was to be in many respects a monotonous voyage, though not altogether without its excitement and stirring incidents. The general manner of our progress was that with which we were now acquainted. We were doomed, as before, to be at intervals stricken by cholera, which seemed to have its favourite lurking-places, generally at the foot of a somewhat precipitous alluvial bank. Night after night rest was disturbed or altogether banished by the sound of tom-toms,. songs, barking of dogs, cries of jackals; sight and smell offended by funeral fires as they blazed in near proximity to us.

More than half our journey was got over without special mishap. Our boatmen observe that signs of coming storm appear in the sky; they prepare as best they can, but soon the hurricane is upon us. Boats are dashed against each other, and against the river bank; waves break over them, tearing away their flimsy gear, battering some to pieces, their inmates obliged to

---

5. *i.e.*, silk produced by the *Antherea paphia*, and allied species.

escape and save themselves as best they could. After a time there came a downpour of rain; then gradually the storm ceased, leaving several of our number boatless, and destitute of greater or smaller portions of our respective kits. Among others, I suffered considerably. A friend in need, more fortunate than myself, gave me hospitality on his boat until sometime thereafter, when, with others similarly situated, I chartered a budgerow. A few days after our mishap news reached us that a similar fleet to our own, with troops,[6] some thirty miles ahead of us, suffered very severely from the same hurricane that had struck us, a considerable number of the men in it having perished in the river.

Without further incident of importance we arrived at Cawnpore in the early days of November, our journey by river having occupied more than two months and a half, the date fourteen years before the terrible year 1857, when that station was to acquire the sad memory ever since associated with it. Anticipating the return to India of the force commanded by General Pollock from Jellalabad, the march to which place had restored British prestige from the temporary eclipse at Jugdulluck. Orders were issued to honour that army by an appropriate military display on the left bank of the Sutlej. Among the regiments assembled for that purpose, at Ferozepore, the then frontier station, were the Buffs. Orders had also directed that on completion of that duty they should inarch towards Allahabad and there occupy the fort, the detachment with which I was connected joining headquarters *en route*. For the time being we were attached to the 50th Regiment, and so continued during the remaining four months of the cold season.

Here took place the first initiation into their several duties connected with regimental life of the young men belonging to our detachment, myself among them. Among the officers in the "Dirty Half-Hundred" who had served with it during the Peninsular War, when, on account of the continuous severe work performed by it, the corps obtained its honourable soubriquet,

---

6. Of the 50th and 62nd Regiments; more than 100 men were lost at Seckreegullee, that being the place where the typhoon occurred.

three[7] remained, looked up to with the respect due to, and then accorded to, distinguished veterans. Alternate with duties assigned to us, amusements filled up our time pleasantly. Gaiety was in full flow. Many were the joyous gatherings by which were filled the Assembly rooms—some years thereafter to be the scene of very terrible doings.

Outdoor games and sports were the order of the day, the tract of jungle in Oude that stretched along the opposite river bank proving our most happy hunting ground. So it was that time passed pleasantly, if in an intellectual sense not very profitably. At the time alluded to traffic and communication with Oude was by means of a long bridge of boats, that bridge from their attack on which in subsequent days the Gwalior mutineers were to be driven by the forces under Sir Colin Campbell.[8]

A large force, comprising all arms, then occupied that important station. The impression made upon us, as for the first time we beheld the magnificent spectacle presented by general field-day parades and exercises, was never to be forgotten. The swarthy visages of the *sepoys*; their quaint uniforms attracted our notice. The solidarity of the 50th gave the impression of irresistible force. The rush of cavalry, as, like a whirlwind, they went at full charge, to a great extent concealed in a cloud of dust raised by their horses' hoofs; the magnificent and unsurpassed Bengal Horse Artillery, in performing the evolutions pertaining to them,—these incidents struck us with amazement and admiration. Little did we think that not many months thereafter we were to be even more struck with admiration at the brilliant performance of some of those very troops in actual fight.

A trip to Agra[9] introduced me to the experiences of *palkee dâk*. Travelling by night, the distance got over was about fifty miles; alongside trotted torch-carriers, the odours from those "pillars of flame" foul and offensive. During the day a halt was made at bungalows provided by Government for the use of trav-

---

7. Colonel Wodehouse, Major Ryan, and Captain Tew.
8. December 28 and 29, 1857.
9. On the invitation of my friend, L. C. Stewart, 39th Regiment.

ellers. Thus were four days occupied in making a journey of two hundred miles. In and near Agra various excursions were made and places of interest visited. In the fort had recently been deposited the gates of Somnath,[10]

I in connection with the removal of which from Ghuznee the bombastic I proclamation by Lord Ellenborough was still subject of comment. The tomb of Akbar[11] and the exquisite Taj Mahal[12] were visited on several occasions. The scene presented by the latter, more especially as seen by moonlight, was extremely beautiful. The minarets and domes of the mausoleum, consisting of pure white marble; the long avenue of cypress trees by which it is approached; the fountains in full play; the ornamental flower pots,—made upon us an impression never afterwards to be forgotten.

With the regiments returned recently from Kandahar, aided by troops from Bombay and Bengal, Sir Charles Napier undertook an expedition against the disaffected Ameers of Scinde. In February, 1843, the battles of Meeanee and Hyderabad ended in defeat of their forces, Hyderabad occupied, the country being conquered during the succeeding month of March. Of that war it was said:

> The Muhamadan rulers of Sind, known as the Ameers, whose chief fault was that they would not surrender their independence, were crushed.

In the neighbouring State of Gwalior events were in progress, the issue of which was destined to affect the 39th, the 50th, and the Buffs in a way not at the moment anticipated by either of those regiments. Early in February, the distant boom of heavy guns intimated to us at Agra that the Maharajah of Gwalior was

---

10. Gates of Somnath—carried thence, A.D. 1024, by the conqueror, Mahmood of Guznee.
11. Akbar the Great, A.D. 1556-1605.
12. Taj Mahal-Bibi ke Roza, or Crown Lady's tomb, erected over the remains of Mumtaz Mahal, the Pride of the Palace, wife of Shah Jehan. She died in childbed of her eighth child, A.D. 1629, at Berhampore in the Deccan, whence her body was carried and buried where the Taj now stands.

dead, and had been succeeded on his throne by his adopted son [13] in the absence of a lineal heir. In such events there did not appear anything to interfere with , the routine of pleasure in which so many young officers indulged; that routine went on uninterruptedly, for as yet with them the serious business of life was in the future.

Those were indeed the days of India's hospitality, alike in respect to individuals and regiments. For example: Three weeks had I been an honorary member of the "Dorsets" mess, when the time of my I departure arrived; yet to my request for my mess bill I received the I reply, "There is none." Among the officers whose hospitality I had so long unconsciously enjoyed were two, father and son, both of whom I was shortly to meet under circumstances very different from those in which I had made their acquaintance.

---

13. The story of these events is concisely given in Sewell's *Analytical History of India*, page 244.

CHAPTER 3

1843. At Allahabad

Eighteen months had elapsed since the day when we left Chatham to that on which we joined the distinguished regiment[1] of which I was a member, the manner of my reception kind and friendly. As the regiment passed through Cawnpore, a short halt was ordered to take place; the camp to be pitched on that part of the parade ground, afterwards to be occupied by the defences in connection with which the story of General Wheeler and his party has left so many sad associations. The object of that halt appeared in Division Orders—the carrying into execution of sentence of death passed by General Court-Martial on a soldier of the regiment convicted of murdering a comrade.

This was to be the first regimental parade on which I was to appear. By sunrise the troops were in their places, so as to form three sides of a square, the fourth being partly occupied by the construction above which the fatal beam and its supports stood prominent. The procession of death began its march, the regimental band wailing forth the Dead March; then came the coffin, carried by low-caste natives; then the condemned man, ghastly pale, strongly guarded. Thus did they proceed until they arrived at the place of execution. The eyes of most of us were averted, and so we saw not the further details of the sad drama. Regiment after regiment marched past the structure, from which dangled the body of a man; thence to their respective barracks or tents, their bands playing "rollicking "tunes.

1. At the time commanded by Colonel Clunie.

Pleasant as novel were the incidents of our march eastward along that most excellent highway, the Grand Trunk Road. The early rouse, "striking" tents, the "fall in," the start while as yet stars glistened in the sky and dawn had not appeared; then came the wild note of the coel [2] as herald of coming day; the gleam of blazing fire far ahead, indicating where the midway halt was to take place, and morning coffee with biscuits was in readiness for all. Resuming the day's journey, we reached the appointed camp ground by 8 a.m. Tents were quickly pitched on lines previously drawn by the quarter-master and his staff. Bath, a hearty breakfast, duty, shooting, and other excursions occupied the day, then early dinner, early to bed, and so ready to undergo similar routine on the morrow. In our progress we I passed through Futtehpore, a place to be subsequently the scene of stubborn fight against mutineers in 1857.

Attached to the Buffs were the remnants of what had been the 44th Regiment, now consisting of a few men of whom the majority were mutilated or suffering from bodily illness; the party under command of Captain Souter, by whose gallant devotion to duty the regimental colour was saved two years previous when our force was annihilated near the Khyber by Affghans, directed by Akbar Khan.

Pârâg, as the locality of Allahabad was anciently called, is closely connected with Hindoo tradition, and still retains a sacred character. At the date referred to in the Ramayana it was a residence of a Rajah of "the powerful Kosalas," whose capital was Ajudyia, their country the modern Oude. Here it was that Rama and Seeta crossed the Ganges in their progress to the jungles of Dandaka, where shortly afterwards she was captured by Ravana and carried away by him to Lunka, otherwise Ceylon.

Within the fort, now occupied by our regiment, is an underground temple dedicated to Siva, its position believed to indicate the point where the mythical Suruswatee joins the still sacred Ganges. On an enclosed piece of ground stands one of six pillars assigned to Asoka, B.C. 240, bearing an inscription of the period

2. Eudynemus Orientalis.

31

of Samudra Gupta, 2nd century A.D. That pillar, having fallen, was restored by Jehangir, A.D. 1605; the fort itself captured by the English from Shah Alum, A.D. 1765.

As the hot season advanced, severe and fatal disease prevailed alarmingly among our men, cholera and heat fever claiming victims after a few hours' illness. Treatment applied by the younger medical officers in accordance with theoretical school teaching was useless, nor was it till the regimental surgeon (Dr. Macqueen) directed us to more practical methods that anything approaching favourable results were attained. In these notes, however, the intention is to omit professional matters.

A full company of our men was sent to Papamow, situated on the right bank of the Ganges, six miles distant, the object being to afford additional space to those within the fort. Captain Airey, in command of the detachment, had been one of the hostages in Affghanistan to Akbar Khan, and utilised on that occasion his culinary talents by acting as cook to the party. For a time the men enjoyed, and benefited by their change to country quarters. Towards the end of the rainy season, however, malarial diseases attacked them to a degree larger in proportion than their comrades in the fort; consequently our detachment was ordered to rejoin Headquarters.

A good deal of freedom was allowed to the soldiers when first sent to the country place above mentioned, one result being that crime was next to absent from among them. A favourite amusement was shooting in the adjoining woods and fields, and, unhappily for some of them, of bathing, notwithstanding strict orders to the contrary, in the Ganges, then in full flood. On one of those shooting excursions a soldier got bitten in the hand by a cobra, the reptile being immediately killed, and brought in with him. That the teeth penetrated was manifest by the wounds; yet, strange to say, no serious results followed—a circumstance accounted for only by supposing that the poison sacs must by some means have been emptied immediately previous. Of those who insisted on entering the river, some fell victims to their temerity.

The pursuit and study of subjects relative to natural history furnished those of us whose leanings were in those directions with continuous enjoyment and profitable occupation. Visits by friends and small attempts at hospitality came in as so many pleasant interludes. When neither of these was practicable, a good supply of books and papers gave us variety in the way of reading.

So time passed until the month of September, when the cultivated fields were covered by heavy crops special to this part of India. A sudden outburst of discordant noises induces us to quit our quarters in search of the wherefore. A dense cloud is seen in rapid advance from the south-east; myriads of locusts, for of those insects it is composed, alight upon and by their accumulated weight bear down the stems to which they cling. Next day a similar flight is upon us, devouring every green thing; eight days thereafter, a third, but it passed over the locality, obscuring the sky as it did so.

The regimental mess house occupied an elevated position adjoining and overlooking the Jumna, a short distance above the confluence of that river with the Ganges, a terrace pertaining to the building being a favourite resort whereon, in the cool of the evening, it was usual for the officers to enjoy the refreshing breeze, when there was any, and contemplate the unrippled surface of the deep stream as it glided past. On one such evening, while a number of us were so enjoying the scene, watching the lights of native boats secured for the night to either bank, and listening to that strange mixture of sounds to which natives give the name of music, a series of what appeared to be floating lamps emerged from where the boats lay thickest and glided along the stream. Here we witnessed the scene alluded to, and so graphically described by L.E.L.[3] in her version of "The Hindoo Girl's Song." (The words are so beautiful and pathetic that I transcribe them below.) It was, in fact, the Dewalee Festival.[4]

---

3. Poor L.E.L.! Further memories of her will recur hereafter.
4. *Dewalee*—Festival to Lakshmi, goddess of wealth and fortune.

Float on, float on, my haunted bark,
Above the midnight tide;
Bear softly o' er the waters dark
The hopes that with thee glide.
Float on, float on, thy freight is flowers,
And every flower reveals
The dreaming of my lonely hours,
The hope my spirit feels.
Float on, float on, thy shining lamp,
The light of love is there;
If lost beneath the waters damp,
That love must then despair.
Float on, beneath the moonlight float,
The sacred billows o' er;
Ah! some kind spirit guards my boat,
For it has gained the shore.

Allahabad was the chief civil station in the provinces; the principal courts were situated there, the higher officials connected with criminal and with revenue administration having their residences scattered over what was an extensive and ornamental settlement. Some of their houses were noted for hospitality, and for more homely entertainments given for the special benefit of the younger officers. Of the latter, that of Mrs. Tayler [5] has left most pleasant recollections, the good influence exerted by that lady making its mark on some of us who might otherwise have had remembrances very different in kind. Among the most esteemed of the residents was Dr. Angus, "The Good Samaritan," as he was called. Hospitable to all; considerate to juniors; his good advice, and help in other ways, readily given to all who in difficulties applied to him.

Early in October, the commander-in-chief, Sir Hugh Gough, arrived *en route* north-westward. New colours were presented by His Excellency to a native regiment (37th) of distinguished service in Affghanistan, the event celebrated by festive gather-

5. Mrs. Tayler, mother of Lady Hope Grant, then a young girl in England at school.

34

ings, in accordance with customary usage. On the staff of His Excellency were two officers, both of whom subsequently attained high military distinction; the one Sir Harry Smith, the other Sir Patrick Grant.

Reports were "in the air" that a Camp of Exercise was about to assemble at Agra, as an experiment then tried in India for the first time. Bazaar report had it that the Buffs were about to be ordered on service, the scene and nature of which did not just then transpire. Meanwhile, responsible officers "saw to" the state of "brown Bess," with which weapon our men were then armed; to that of ammunition, and other necessary items of equipment. The arrival of part of the 29th Regiment, to take our place, next followed, and, simultaneously, came an order directing the Buffs to proceed to Kalpee, on the Jumna, thirteen days' march distant. A few days thereafter, published orders directed the organization of "the Army of Exercise" into divisions and brigades; still, there was no inkling of what was about to happen.

For some time previous evidences were manifest that all was not right in Gwalior; latterly report said that things in that State had settled down, terms having been come to between the young Maharajah and leaders of the disaffected. A few days thereafter, our preparations were renewed; our weakly men, together with soldiers' wives and children, arranged for to be left behind, and with a fighting strength of 739 powerful and seasoned soldiers, the regiment started fit and ready for whatever service might be required of it.

The actual state of affairs, above referred to, was briefly this:—

The young Maharajah, known as "Ali Jah Jyajee Scindia," owed his selection to the widow of the deceased monarch of the same name, who died childless, she a girl aged thirteen, named Tara Bye. To the post of Regent, Mama Sahib, an uncle of the deceased monarch, was acknowledged by Lord Ellenborough through the Resident, against the wishes of the Maharanee; Dada Khasjee, steward of the Household, by the Maharanee. Thereupon, the Resident was ordered by His Excellency to quit Gwalior, and the Dada prepared his troops to oppose forces of the Company, if sent against him; hence the campaign now about to take place.

In the Punjab, conditions were at the same time most serious, giving rise to expectations of armed intervention there. For example:—

On the 15th of September, 1843, was perpetrated the double murder of the Maharajah Shere Singh[6] and his son Pertab, at the northern gate of Lahore, the conspiracy which led up to that deed having been formed by Dyhan Singh.[7] Next day Ajeet Singh, by whose hand the crime was committed, together with his followers, were attacked and put to death by Heera Singh, son of the deceased *vizier*, and his party. For a time a state of anarchy, with its attendant slaughter and rapine, prevailed within the capital.

These having run their course, Dhuleep Singh, only surviving son of Runjeet, was placed upon the throne of his father, Heera Singh making himself *vizier*. Meanwhile, the Sikh or Khalasa army had become formidable under Lai Singh, a favourite of the Ranee;[8] as an outcome of a conspiracy among them, Heera was murdered, his place taken by Lai.[9] Nothing could then restrain their ardour but an expedition into British territory, for which it was well understood that preparations were in progress. The proceedings thus alluded to supplied ample subject for comment in the papers, and talk at social gatherings.

---

6. Shere Singh, an unacknowledged son of Runjeet, "the Lion of the Punjab."
7. Dyhan Singh, *vizier* of the above.
8. The Ranee Jinda, mother of Dhuleep. She was now Regent.
9. Subsequently Sikh commander at the battle of Ferozeshah, December 21, 1845.

CHAPTER 4

1843-1844. Campaign in Gwalior

On the day the Buffs began their march, I proceeded to join the 16th Lancers, to which distinguished regiment I had been, by General Orders, attached for duty. Ten nights were passed in travelling by *palkee dâk*. In early morning of the eleventh day the Kutub was seen in bold relief against the indistinct horizon, for the atmosphere was laden with dust. After a little time, the Jumna was crossed by a bridge of boats; then another interval, and I was hospitably received by Dr. Ross, to whom I had an introduction.

Various places of interest in the imperial city were visited in turn. The Jumna Musjid, or chief mosque, its domes and minarets imposing in their grandeur; the balcony in the Chandee Chouk, whereon, in 1739, Nadir Shah sat witnessing the massacre of the inhabitants; the palace of the once "Great Mogul"; the smaller building in its garden, within which had stood "the Peacock Throne"; the remnants of the crystal seat upon which, in ancient times, monarchs were crowned; those of numerous fountains; the Persian inscription, to the effect that *If there is an Elysium upon earth, it is this*. But from the ruins around, frogs and lizards stared at us; the once gorgeous palaces, and all that pertained to them, were smeared over with filth.

At a distance of twelve miles from the city stands the Kutub, surrounded by numerous remains of buildings, the road through all that way being along a space covered by ruins of various kinds. The Cashmere gate of Delhi by which we emerged was then noted as the place where Mr. Fraser, Resident at the Court of the Emperor, was murdered, and where Shumshoodeen, the instigator of that crime, was executed; it was to become famous as the scene of severe but victorious struggle against the mutineers in 1857.

About two miles onwards stood the ruins of an astronomical observatory, one of two of their kind in India, the other being at Benares. A little farther on was the tomb of Sufter Jung, minister to the princes of Delhi; then continuous ranges of ruins until we arrive at Feroze's Lath, a metal pillar, the history of which is somewhat obscure, but on which marks of shot indicate attempts by Nadir Shah to destroy it. Now we reach the Kutub, a pillar sixty-five yards in circumference at the base, the ascent within it comprising three hundred and twenty-nine steps, the exterior interrupted by four terraces. Legend relates that it is Hindoo in origin; history that its exterior ornamentation was seriously damaged by the Mahometan conquerors. Not far from it are the ruins of what would seem to have been a tower of still larger dimensions. In the vicinity of the latter a deep well, into which from a height of sixty feet natives dived, performing strange evolutions in mid-air as they did so.

From Delhi to Muttra the journey was made along by-paths across country. In camp near the latter-named city were the 16th, commanded by Colonel Cureton, and there I joined them. The fact had meantime been promulgated that the destination of "the Army of Exercise" was to be Gwalior. The force so named, 30,000 strong, was to be divided into two wings or corps, to enter that State simultaneously from two directions. That from the south and eastward comprised the Buffs, 50th Regiment, 9th Lancers, artillery, native cavalry, and native infantry; that from the west, the 16th Lancers, 39th and 40th Regiments, a strong force of artillery, 1st and 10th Regiments of Native Cavalry, 4th Irregulars, and several regiments of native infantry.

While arrangements for active movements were being matured, those of us on whom as yet cares of office had not descended, passed our time in visiting places of interest in and near the cities of Muttra and Bindrabund, both held sacred by Hindoos in relation to the life of Krishna. In the last-named city we were only permitted to approach the principal temple that stood close to its entrance gate, but from the distance we could see, stretching far away as it seemed to us, the vista of its interior, dimly lighted by hanging lamps; at its extreme end the emblem of the deity to whom it was dedicated, resplendent with gems and precious stones. Everywhere along the narrow streets and from the flat roofs of their houses armies of "sacred" baboons grinned and chattered at us. A picnic to some characteristically Indian gardens[1] adjoining the banks of the Jumna furnished us with another pleasant interlude.

The division of the force of which the 16th were part resumed its march; in three days arrived at its assigned position not far from Agra: and there encamped, pending the result of an ultimatum dispatched by the Governor-General to the disaffected Gwalior leaders. Meanwhile, arrivals of the high civil and military officials, additions to the force, salutes and festivities afforded all of us pleasant occupation and variety.

The answer of the chiefs arrives; its terms are defiant. War against the State immediately proclaimed[2] by Lord Ellenborough; portions of the force put in motion towards the river Chumbul, among them the 16th. The appointed rendezvous near Dholpore is speedily reached and there we encamp.

A *vakeel* arrives in camp, bearer of a dispatch by which the leaders of Gwalior rebels submit proposals for peace, on their own terms. They are at once refused. By daybreak next morning the force is in motion. Three hours suffice for crossing the Chumbul, an operation effected without important incident; establishments follow without delay; camp is pitched on hostile territory. The aspect of our position and immediate vicinity presents uneven ground, intersected by deer ravines, destitute of roadways.

Our halt is of short duration. Early next morning the force

---

1. Belonging to Luckimchund, at one time a Government contractor.
2. December 20, 1843.

emerged on open country; in due time arrived in near proximity to the village of Sehoree, and there encamped.

Meanwhile, information was received that Gwalior forces were rapidly concentrating in our front. Officers on the staff of our quartermaster general reconnoitred the country to a radius of ten miles and more around our camp. Soon the "Chief"[3] issued orders that the march should be resumed next day, and the Mahrattas attacked if met with.

Conversation at mess turned upon the probable events so soon to transpire; extemporised plans by individual officers indicated the several views they entertained of what was to happen. The very young expressed hopes that the enemy would show good fight; some of their number speculated on the chances of promotion before them. Then broke in one of the seniors, who had gained experience of war in Afghanistan: "I have just been employed in making a few little arrangements in case of accidents."

"Highly proper," remarked another "for no one knows what tomorrow may bring forth."

At daylight on December 29 our force began its advance, its manner of distribution to make an attack simultaneously on front and flank of the position known to have been occupied by the Mahrattas the previous evening. But during the night they had taken up a new position, considerably in advance, and from it unexpectedly opened fire on our leading columns. The general force was at once directed upon the new position. Horse Artillery commanded by Captain Grant[4] at full gallop rode directly at the Gwalior battery; opened fire upon it with crushing effect, and within the space of a few minutes reduced it to silence. Having done so, away again at full gallop Captain Grant led his battery against one on the left of the former that had meanwhile opened upon us, our infantry columns plodding their way, slowly but steadily, against its line of fire.

---

3. Sir Hugh Gough.

4. Charley Grant Sahib, as he continued to be called many years afterwards when as a General Officer he commanded a Division.

Very soon that battery also was silenced. The infantry were at work with the bayonet with terrible effect upon the enemy, with very heavy loss to our own forces, in men, horses, and ammunition. A third battery began its deadly work upon other bodies of infantry, in motion onwards. Again Captain Grant led his troop against it with the same result; then arrived the infantry, including the 39th and 40th British regiments; then hand-to-hand conflict, and then—the positions were in the grasp of our forces.

While thus the conflict raged fiercely, the 16th, led by Colonel Rowland Smyth,[5] together with the two cavalry regiments[6] brigaded with them, were ordered to sweep round the rebel camp, cut off, destroy, or disperse those who, driven from their guns, might take to flight. The lancers dashed onwards at the charge, the bright steel and showy pennants of their weapons seeming to skim the ground, while at intervals stray rebels fell lifeless. The Gwalior men, anticipating such a manoeuvre, had taken precautions against its complete success; the position for heaviest guns selected by them had along its front a ravine of great breadth and depth.

Upon its edge the cavalry suddenly came, nor is it clear by what means they escaped being precipitated into it. There was for a moment some confusion as the halt was sounded; eighteen guns directly in front, six others in flank sent their missiles through our ranks or high above them. To remain exposed to risks of more perfect practice would serve no good purpose; there was no alternative but to retire. The infantry were seen advancing; down one side of the ravine, lost to sight; up the further side, then onwards, into the batteries, and then—the fight was won.

When at first the 16th took the position assigned to them on the field, it may have been that my endeavours to discover what was subsequently called "the first line of assistance" were unsuccessful; it may have been that they were not very keenly made,

---

5. Colonel Cureton now acted as Brigadier in command of the cavalry.
6. 10th Bengal and 4th Irregular Cavalry.

at any rate "the Brigadier"—for so was named the troop horse I rode—knew his right place in the ranks, and so enabled me to witness the events now described.

Returning to my proper duties, I joined the parties who traversed the field of battle in search of wounded. Great, alas! was the number who lay prostrate,—many dead, many more suffering from wounds. Among the latter was General Churchill, his injuries of a nature to make him aware that speedy death was inevitable. While being attended to with all possible care, he requested me to take charge of the valuable watch he wore, and after his demise to send it to his son-in-law, Captain Mitchell[7] of the 6th Foot, at that time serving in South Africa. During the night he died, and his request was carried out by me.

At a short distance lay, in the growing crop that covered the field of battle, Lieutenant Cavanagh of the 4th Irregulars, loudly calling to attract attention, supporting by his hands a limb from which dangled the foot and part of the leg, his other limb grazed by a round shot which inflicted both wounds, and passed through his horse, now lying dead beside him. He was taken to the hospital tents, where meanwhile wounded soldiers and officers in considerable numbers had accumulated. The surgeons' work begun, three[8] of us mutually assisted each other.

The turn of Lieutenant Cavanagh to be attended to having come, he made a request that we should "just wait a bit while he wrote to his wife," for he had recently been married. This done, he submitted to amputation, and during that process uttered no cry or groan, though nothing in the shape of anaesthetic was given, nor had chloroform as such been discovered; then, during the interval purposely permitted to elapse between the operation and final dressing, he continued his letter to his young wife, these circumstances illustrating the courage and endurance so characteristic among men (and women) at the time referred to. His case was one of many men who had to be succoured that day.

---

7. Afterwards General Sir John Mitchell, G.C.B.
8. Namely, Dr. Walker of the Body Guard, Currie of 16th Lancers, and myself.

Meanwhile the force was in process of encamping on the field so gallantly won; the 16th paraded for roll call, the band of the regiment playing "The Convent Bells," the notes of which long years thereafter recalled the day and occasion. Casualties[9] among the men were only nine; but among the horses more numerous than they had been at Waterloo, whereas Light Dragoons the 16th so highly distinguished themselves.[10]

The arduous and responsible work of the day over, those of us who could do so withdrew to our tents, our hearts full of gratitude to the Almighty for individual safety, there to obtain such measure of rest and quiet as under the circumstances was procurable; for all through the evening and early hours of night the bright glare from burning villages, the dense smoke from others, the dull heavy sound of exploding mines made the hours hideous. Such was the battle of "Maharajpore."

During the evening the mangled remains of what in the morning had been a band of brave men were committed to earth. With returning daylight the same sad task was continued, all possible honour being shown to the dead according to the rank they had held, from that of General Officer in the person of General Churchill, who had succumbed in the course of the night, to that of the private soldier. Meantime, in tents the work of attending to the wounded went steadily on. There, officers and men whom we personally knew, lay helpless; among them Major Bray, of the 39th, and his son in adjoining cots, the former terribly burnt by the explosion of a mine, the life-blood of the latter ebbing through a bullet-wound in his chest.[11] And there

---

9. The strength of the opposing forces at the commencement of battle was: British, 14,000, with forty guns; Mahrattas, 18,000, including 3,000 cavalry and 100 guns. The losses were: British, 106 killed, 648 wounded, seven missing; total, 797. Seven officers were killed on the field or died of wounds. The Mahrattas sustained losses estimated at 3,000 to 4,000.

10. In repulsing a body of French lancers in pursuit of a party of Scots Greys, for which, as marks of appreciation by the king, they were made lancers and granted scarlet uniform.

11. Many years thereafter I became acquainted with Colonel Bray, who obtained his commission "without purchase" in acknowledgment of services rendered by his father and brother.

were many other very painful instances, to the aid of whom our best endeavours had to be directed.

It was for the time being impossible to carry on with the army, in its further advance, the large number of wounded with which it was now encumbered. A guard sufficiently strong to protect the extemporised field hospital having been detailed, the general force resumed its march, the intention being to press on as rapidly as possible to the capital. Along a tract of soft sandy country, oppressed by heat, exhausted by the fatigue of the previous day, the troops plodded their weary way, in their progress passing many relics of the recent fight, including shot, arms, shreds of clothing, dead bodies of animals and of men, etc.

At last the halt resounded from trumpet and bugle; for a time we rested as best we could, and then the tents having arrived we encamped. Some further delay was rendered necessary by circumstances. During that and the succeeding day information was received in camp that while the battle was proceeding in the vicinity of Maharajpore, an engagement equally formidable took place between the Mahrattas and the force under General Grey at Punniar, on the eastern border of the Gwalior State; that in it the Buffs had sustained a loss in killed of one officer and thirteen men, in wounded of three officers and sixty men,—the casualties in the 50th being equally numerous.

The arrival in camp of the Queen Regent, together with her *Sirdars*, and the young Maharajah, the salute on the accession of whom some ten months previous has been already mentioned, caused no little excitement, and at the same time much speculation among us. Later on, however, the report spread that the result of their interview with the Governor-General was by both parties deemed satisfactory.

As some among us took rides in different directions around our camp, not an armed man was met with. In some of the villages visited individuals who had escaped the carnage of the previous day were found lying more or less completely stripped of clothing, and wounded, some of them dead. The villagers had fallen upon the fugitives, robbed them of all they possessed, then turned them adrift. They had failed, and they paid the penalty of failure.

The march resumed, the force in due time reached the immediate vicinity of Gwalior, and there encamped. The huge fortress seemed to tower above us, while the neighbouring hills looked as if from their summits a well-directed fire could have swept the country to a considerable distance around. Within a couple of days arrived the force under General Grey and the Seepree contingent under Brigadier Stubbs. Negotiations had so far advanced that the latter took possession of the fort, the camp of the former adding very considerably to the dimensions of the great canvas city already existing. Rapidly and completely did the routine of life to which for some time past we had been accustomed undergo a change: complimentary visits and entertainments, each regiment entertaining everyone else and being in turn entertained by them. By the high officials durbars and receptions were held, to which ceremonials Representatives of Gwalior having given their presence, the fact that they did so indicated that the end of our expedition was approaching.

Connected with the strong fortress by which the city of Gwalior is dominated were many points of interest; among them the general aspect of decay as seen from without, the tortuous narrow lane that leads to it, the steep and difficult flight of stone steps by which the ascent must be made, and powerful gates that seemed to lead but to a mass of ruins. Within the defences we were face to face with remains of temples, pillars, and arches pertaining to edifices of the Jains;[12] there were remains of what had been reservoirs of large dimensions and beautiful workmanship, in some portions of which clear water glistened in the sunlight. Only one piece of ordnance was met with; it was an ancient gun, seventeen feet in length, and apparently capable of discharging a fifty-eight pound shot.

The process of disarming the Gwalior troops was next performed—somewhat slowly at first, and not without some risk

---

12. *Jains.* The origin of the sect of Buddhists so called dates from sixth or seventh century A.D., its decay in the twelfth or thirteenth

of difficulty, but more rapidly as information circulated among them that they were to receive all arrears of pay due, and a certain number of them taken into the service of "the Company." [13] Then did they march to the places assigned to them in battalions, their bands playing what was intended to be "God Save the Queen"; finally laying down their arms and surrendering their colours, all of which, packed on elephants, were taken to the fort. The artillery and cavalry gave theirs up elsewhere.

The wounded from different regiments were collected in camp, those among them fit to undergo the journey towards Allahabad being dispatched thither by means of *doolies* and native carts (*hackeries*),—the orders of the commander-in-chief, as expressed by himself, being that their progress thither should be by "easy stages and intermediate halts." From Allahabad they were to be conveyed by means of native boats to Calcutta, and there embarked on board one or more of the most comfortably and well-equipped ships proceeding *via* the Cape to England. For those whose condition was more serious, accommodation was provided in camp, and in public buildings outside the city of Gwalior. Among those so left were three respected officers of the Buffs.

Of these, Captain Chatterton and Dr. Macqueen shortly afterwards succumbed to the disease—induced by the trials of active service. The death of the third—namely, Captain Magrath— was attended by a little circumstance which showed that the spirit of romance persisted to the last in him. During the battle at Punniar, he, together with thirteen men of his company, were blown up by the explosion of a tumbril that they were in the act of capturing. Captain Magrath and twelve of the soldiers with him speedily succumbed, or were instantly killed.

When his body was being prepared for burial, there, over the region of the heart, was found a lady's glove; nor was it difficult, bearing in mind some of the most pleasant incidents at Allahabad already recorded, to indicate the hand to which the memento

---

13. The "Gwalior Contingent" so established joined the mutineers in 1857, and took prominent part in the investment of Cawnpore.

originally pertained.

A general parade of the combined forces now took place. On that occasion the young Maharajah accompanied the Governor-General, by whom, in the course of his address, sufficient was expressed to raise hopes that further service on the Punjab frontier was to be immediately undertaken. But this was not to be.

Disintegration of "the Army of Exercise" forthwith began, in obedience to orders issued. Starting on their return march, the 16th traversed the field on which, twenty-nine days previous, the battle already mentioned had taken place. At short distances over its extent lay bodies of men and horses far advanced in decomposition; fragments of natives and equipments everywhere. The village of Maharajpore reduced to charred ruins; in their midst numbers of dead bodies of those who had so manfully stood their ground and perished as they did so. In what had been a room or enclosure a confused heap of what had been men further testified to the obstinacy of the defence. In some places miserable-looking inhabitants were searching among the ruins for property and houses. Such was the wreck of battle.

Thence to Meerut the march of the lancers was uneventful. Halts for a day were made respectively at Hattras and Alighur, associated as those places are with early campaigns of the century. At the latter fortress we visited the gate and approach thereto through which was made the historic charge by the 76th Regiment; [14] then the monument to officers and men who fell on that occasion, and at Laswaree soon thereafter. Twenty days *en route;* the 16th re-enter Meerut, whence they had started on service now happily performed. Very touching were meetings between wives and their husbands; though to younger and less thoughtful men the full significance of husband and father restored to those dependent on him had yet to be realized.

A series of entertainments, including regimental dinners and a station ball, welcomed the return to cantonments of the 16th and troop of Horse Artillery, now under Captain Alexander, that had so much distinguished itself at Maharajpore. Preparations

---

14. Under Lord Lake, September 3, 1803.

rapidly pushed on for the annual race for "the Lancer Cup," and all seemed to settle down for the hot season of 1844, then fast approaching.

A young (artillery) officer had the indiscretion to write to the papers a severe criticism—from his point of view—on the tactics to which, according to himself, was due the heavy cost in which the recent victory had been gained. A second officer made open boast of the help he had given in preparing that letter, and both of them boasted pretentiously of what they had done. But soon the attention of the "authorities," including the venerable commander-in-chief, was drawn to the comments in question, with the result to the subalterns concerned that, as expressed at the time, they were "come down upon like a sledge-hammer." Popular verdict declared that the example set by them, if followed, would destroy all discipline.

The date on which, according to ancient custom, the great Hindoo religious festival of the year was to be held at Hurdwar was near at hand. As on similar occasions, arrangements were made to send to that place a small body of native troops, those detailed for the purpose being men of the 53rd Native Infantry and 10th Cavalry, I placed in departmental charge. Our march thither began in the middle of March. As we proceeded, we went along through a highly cultivated country, many of the fields covered with "golden grain," for it was the season of barley harvest. More and more distinct became the snowy peaks and precipices of the Himalayahs; denser and more dense the masses of pilgrims toiling their weary way to the sacred shrine, for the occasion was that of the greater fair known as Kumbh Mela, held every twelfth year.[15]

Situated directly on the right bank of the Ganges, where that river emerges from the Himalayahs, the surroundings of Hurdwar are extremely beautiful, comprising hill, valley, forest, and

15. The festival takes place on the first day of the (Hindoo) month Baishakh, that is, commencement of the Solar year (March-April) and anniversary of the day on which the river Ganges first appeared on earth. Every twelfth year the planet Jupiter being in Aquarius, a feast of peculiar sanctity occurs; the great bathing day, or Maha Mela, coinciding with the new moon.

stream. At short intervals temples stand; *ghats* or steps that lead downward to the sacred stream are crowded with devotees. In the clear, rapid stream, men, women, children, and fish commingle—for, like the river, the fish are sacred. The hills immediately behind the town are of the Sewalik range. Along their face occur a series of what were roads, though now scarcely deserving the name; on either side of them are veritable rock dwellings, now occupied by Fakeers. To the geologist the same range has interest connected with the remains of extinct animals contained therein; among them, of Ganesa's elephant, that lived, died, and became imbedded in marshes subsequently to be upheaved and so form the range referred to.

On this occasion [16] an estimated number of two hundred thousand persons were assembled on and in the immediate neighbourhood of the *ghats* to take part in what was called "the great celebration." At a given signal by the Brahmin priests, the masses precipitated themselves into the river, there to perform their religious ceremonies. Of the number who did so, about fifteen thousand were women; but it was said that during some previous years female devotees had been fewer than heretofore. After nightfall the river was illuminated by floating lamps as already described in reference to the Jumna at Allahabad, the scene presented being, as on that occasion, very beautiful.

An excursion to a distance of twenty miles or so up the valley of the Dhoon, undertaken for the combined purposes of shooting small game and relaxation, introduced us to surroundings very beautiful in themselves, full also of living things, animal and vegetable, most interesting to lovers of Nature. From the point reached by us a striking view was obtained of the ranges on which stand respectively the sanatoria of Landour and Mussoorie, and in the further distance snow-covered peaks of the Himalayahs.

The *mela,* or festival, over, without mishap or outbreak of special sickness, our return march took place. The midday heat had become great; we were therefore glad to be again within

16. April 11.

comfortable houses at Meerut, provided with *thermantadotes* and *tatties*;[17] and so the temperature reduced from 105^0 F. in the open to 76° F. indoors.

Not long thereafter the greater number, if indeed not all of us, were gratified on reading, in Government Orders, the announcement that officers and men who had been present at the battles of Meeanee or Hyderabad, recently fought in Scinde, Punniar, or Maharajpore in Gwalior, were granted as a donation one years' *batta*, amounting in my instance, with relative rank of lieutenant, to *Rs*.700—a very welcome windfall.

Certain native regiments were at this time ordered to the first-named country. Rumour spread that peace having been established therein, the extra allowances granted to troops while war was in progress was to be discontinued. In the regiments alluded to insubordination immediately showed itself, in at least one of them to a degree bordering on mutiny. A general parade was ordered; the disaffected corps so placed as to be in face of artillery, on either side cavalry and infantry; thereupon the *sepoys* belonging to it laid down their arms, after which they were paid up to date and escorted out of the station. The officer commanding another corps took upon himself to get rid of the ringleaders without waiting for official authority for so doing. Thus was suppressed what for the moment threatened to become a somewhat difficult state of matters. This was in 1844. The terrible events of 1857 at the same station were in the future.

The state of unrest with reference to affairs in the Punjab continued to increase, the likelihood of war next cold season appearing the greater from the facts that military stores were ordered to be collected at Umballah and Ferozepore, means of transport arranged for, and troops of various arms warned to proceed towards the frontier. Meanwhile, Lord Ellenborough was recalled, and Lord Hardinge reigned as Governor-General in his stead.

At the end of April, in obedience to orders, I started away to rejoin the Buffs, who had returned to Allahabad. The first part

17. Prepared from the roots of *Andropogon*.

of the journey thither was performed by horse transit, then recently introduced—the *palanquin* placed upon a four-wheeled truck or cart, drawn by a single horse at the rate of seven miles per hour; for as yet railways had not been introduced into India. The latter part of the journey was by ordinary "*palkee dâk*"; and so, in due course, I was again with the happy regiment to which properly I belonged.

CHAPTER 5

1844-1845. Allahabad to England

Routine of duty, and responsibilities connected with what was called "full charge" of the regiment, now devolved upon me. Much had to be learnt in respect to official matters relating to my new position, nor could it be so except from so-called "subordinates "attached in those days to hospitals pertaining to British troops; to them. I had, therefore, to refer, and from them gain needed information.

The aspect of cantonments during the next few months much resembled that of the previous hot season: pleasure and gaiety at suitable times, but not to interfere with duty. Among the soldiers unhappily there occurred, as before, great sickness and mortality, the line of new-made graves in the cemetery filled the previous year, and then numbering sixty, being duplicated and exceeded by one on this occasion.

Late in September, orders of readiness to proceed to Calcutta, there to embark for England, were appreciated in different senses by the younger officers and by the older, the latter contrasting in their minds their relative rates of pay in India, where the *rupee* had its standard value, and at home. With few exceptions the juniors expressed themselves as delighted at the prospect.

Then came the customary order that, prior to its departure, men who so desired should be given the opportunity to volunteer from the regiment to certain specified corps whose period of service in India had yet some years to run. A special officer was appointed to superintend the proceeding. Applicants for the privilege were subjected to physical examination; their defaulter sheets and "small books" looked at, after which, if deemed eligible, and under forty years of age, they were accepted, and received a bounty equivalent in amount to £3 sterling. To those whose age exceeded that limit no bounty was officially given, but a corresponding sum was granted from regimental funds as they existed at the time. As an unfortunate part of the system the canteen was kept open throughout; there the bounty money was quickly spent, with the result that throughout the week devoted to "volunteering" scenes of irregularity became numerous; parades and discipline were in abeyance, drunkenness and riot took their places.

As the arrival of our regiment, and its return from active service, had been made the occasion for a round of entertainments, so was now its prospective departure; civil officials and officers of native regiments joined in turn to show attention to the Buffs, and thus testify good fellowship and friendly sentiments towards the corps. Then came the final official ordeal; namely, inspection by the venerable officer commanding the Division. General Watson, then said to be of the old school, had seen much war service; personally amiable, but so full of years that, on the occasion of the parade in question, he was unable to mount a horse, and so perforce witnessed the formality of the march past while he remained on foot.

Boats of the kinds already described now lay ready moored to the bank of the Jumna for our reception. The general gave as a last entertainment a sumptuous *dejeûner*, to which were invited the principal officers, civil and military, of the station. Healths proposed and drunk to in champagne; good wishes expressed; leave-takings gone through; then all take their respective places; bands play "Auld lang syne," "The girls we left behind us," "Home, sweet home," etc.; we are speedily on board; the moorings untied; the "fleet" in movement with the placid stream; from the ramparts of the fort heavy guns fire a "Royal salute" in honour of our regiment. Thus begins the journey homewards.[1]

---

1. October 16, 1844.

We are speedily at the fort of Chunar, built by the Mahomedan conquerors of India, from Hindoo temples destroyed for
that purpose; captured by Major—afterwards Sir Hector Monro
in 1764,[2] but still held semi-sacred by the descendants of those
whose shrines were so desecrated. On an open tract of ground
in its near vicinity, a series of barracks and small houses were occupied by pensioners of the East India Company.

Benares, viewed from the Ganges, is picturesque, and in some
respects beautiful. Houses of red sandstone, their fanciful windows, projecting balconies, and flat roofs, giving to them a character all their own. The city extends from the very edge of the
river; its numerous temples and *ghats*—the latter crowded with
devotees and others, wearing garments of many colours, giving
the scene a picturesque aspect. Some of the temples and *ghats*
present a dilapidated appearance; but others, especially that of
Visheswar—dedicated to Siva—is resplendent with gold gilding.
Another striking object is the Mosque of Arungzebe, erected in
the reign of that monarch from Hindoo temples destroyed for
that purpose. Near the golden temple, in the heart of the- city,
is the no less famous well, named after Manic Karnik, believed by
votaries to be filled with "the *sudor* of Vishnu," and at its bottom
to contain Truth. At a short distance is the Astronomical Observatory, erected by Jai Singh, A.D. 1693.

History records that this ancient city continued during many
generations to be the metropolis of Aryan "civilization in India.
It was at Sarnath, a suburb of Kasi, as Benares was then called,
that in the sixth century B.C. Gautama preached the doctrines of
Karma[3] and Nirvana.[4] There Buddhism assumed its sway, which
it retained till the fourth century A.D., when it gave way before
a revival of Hindooism, in regard to which religion Benares has
ever since been considered its most sacred city.

Here we first witnessed the celebration of the Ramdeela festival It consists in a representation of the more important incidents connected with the abduction of Sita; the chase, the siege,

---

2. Or rather, fell into his hands as a result of his victory at Buxar.
3. That each act in this life bears its fruit in the next.
4. The attainment of a sinless state of existence.

and capture of Ravanu's stronghold; her rescue, the ordeal of fire, to test her purity, and reception by Rama. As noted at the time, the performances, interpreted by the light of legend, gave to them considerable interest.

Resuming our river journey, we met a fleet of boats similar to our own, having on board a party of the 29th Regiment, in progress towards the north-west. The effective portion of the regiment was marching to its destination from Ghazepore, at which place it had been stationed during the two years it had been in India. From a strength of close upon 1,200, it had been in that short time reduced, by fever and cholera, to little over 400 effectives. Alas! out of those remaining, great were to be the losses at Ferozeshah, and other frontier battles, then in the near future.

There was nothing in the aspect of Ghazepore, or the buildings connected with it, to account for the havoc in life and health sustained by the 29th Regiment. A large extent of grass-covered plain separates the station proper from the river. On it stands a monument, erected in memory of Lord Cornwallis,[5] who died near this place, while in progress up the Ganges. That monument, surrounded by tamarisk bushes, above which its summit rises, bears upon it a memorial figure by Flaxman.

The range of barracks and the church are the only other buildings that are immediately seen. A visit to the native town brought us to the ruins of what had been the palace of Mir Cossim Ali Khan, whose forces were defeated, and power destroyed, at Buxar, in 1764, by Major Munro. The graceful proportion of its pillars, arches, and general aspect struck us forcibly, though the building itself is in a state of decay, as are also the numerous smaller ranges by which, in former days, it was surrounded; nor is it more than eighty years since that decay began. Other points of interest connected with Ghazepore include the growth and manufacture of poppy and opium, roses and their otto. A breeding stud for cavalry and artillery horses is here maintained by Government.

5. Died 1805.

Buxar, our next halting place, was one of three places at which breeding studs were maintained by "the Company," the other two being Ghazepore, already mentioned, and Haupur. It would appear, however, that all these are insufficient to meet the requirements of the army, and that consequently importation of horses from the Cape and Australia has had to be resorted to.

Dinapore, then occupied by European[6] artillery, one British and three native regiments of infantry, for the assigned purpose of guarding against possible incursion by the Nepaulese, whose relations towards the Government of India were somewhat strained. It was said that for a number of years the terms of the Treaty of 1816 between Sir David Ochterlony and the chief of the Ghoorkas were faithfully adhered to by the latter; but that in recent times signs of disaffection had begun to show themselves. As an outcome of the Treaty in question, some of the Nepaulese took military service under the Company, they being enrolled in what became known as Ghoorka regiments. For some reason, the nature of which did not transpire, several days elapsed before our journey was resumed.

Impressions of the place were not particularly favourable; that it has attractions of a kind, however, seems evident, as families and various retired officers were said to make it their residence. A few miles distant is the city of Patna—Pataliputra of the Hindoos, and Palibothra of the Greeks—famous in relation to British history as the scene of murder by Kossim Khan, in 1763, of 200 Englishmen, besides 2,000 *sepoys*; to become again noted in connection with events of 1857. On our way to and from that city we noticed by the roadside the now disused grain store, erected in 1769-70, to receive grain against the great famine then prevailing in Behar, in respect to which it is related that

> the tanks were dried up, the springs ceased to reach the surface, and within the first nine months of 1770 one-third of the population of Lower Bengal were carried off

6. During the early wars by the East India Company the troops employed by it comprised men of various European nationalities, besides natives of the United Kingdom.

by want of food.

The 62nd, occupying barracks at Dinapore, entertained the officers of the Buffs on a scale of hospitality and in a manner to be compared only with regimental festivities pictured in the works of Charles Lever. "The Springers," as in those days they loved to be called, were under orders for Umballah, much delighted at prospects of service therein implied; for the state of affairs in the Punjab, already mentioned, had from day to day continued to increase in gravity. The feeling of gallant hilarity was expressed in a somewhat demonstrative manner in extemporary song by one of their officers in early morning hours, while mess had not yet broken up.[7] Of our festive hosts on that occasion scarcely one was alive fourteen months thereafter.

Resuming our journey, our fleet was moored about sunset under a somewhat high alluvial bank, such as in this part of the river course are of frequent occurrence. To several of our soldiers the result was fatal; during the night cholera attacked with violence, and claimed them as victims. As we continued on our way next day the malady seemed to be left behind us.

Monghyr, at which we speedily arrived, is interesting in several respects. To the cession of its rather imposing fort was immediately ascribed the massacre of our countrymen at Patna, as already mentioned. Near this place, in the year of that occurrence, 1763, a mutiny occurred, in which not only native but also European troops were concerned, nor was it until several of their number had been blown from guns by order of Major Munro, already mentioned, that the outbreak was suppressed.

At this place more hospitality was shown us. While yet at some distance from our halting ground, an invitation reached the regiment from Mr. Hodson, then occupying the position

---

7. The officer alluded to, familiarly known as "Paddy" Graves, parodied a well-known soldiers' song of Peninsular days after this manner:—

The Sixty-second Springers all—are
Going to march unto Umballah—r;
And the Buffs, that gallant band—are
Going to their native land—are.
Love, farewell.

of Joint Magistrate and Collector, that officers should dine with him; while to the soldiers, "refreshments" would be served on tables arranged for the purpose as near as possible to the boats. Thus did our host express the compliment he desired to show the regiment, and very highly were his successful endeavours appreciated.

Our next halting place was Bhaugulpore. There, in 1827, the Buffs were stationed, while as yet our frontier line was comparatively little advanced,—Bhurtpore only the previous year captured. In the range of hills that thence extend in a south-westerly direction are various wild Santhal tribes, very low in civilization, devil-worshippers by custom;[8] their weapons were chiefly bows and arrows; their own ethnic alliance believed to be Dravidian.

At the time referred to the number of steamers on the Ganges was small; the length of inland voyage from three to four weeks. Officers and others availing themselves of that mode of transit considered that they were travelling "by express." It was customary with some to spend the period of sick leave, extending in certain instances to six months, on board comfortably fitted up "*budgerows*" on the river; tradesmen also arranged the kind of boat so called as travelling shops, and these different classes of persons and craft gave certain variety to our river voyage. Arrived at Rajmahal, the former capital of Northern Bengal, but now a ruined mass out of which stood a few broken shafts of what had been pillars of black marble. The ruined palace dates back only to A.D. 1630. Sultan Shujah, by whom it was founded, elder brother of Arungzebe, was at the time Governor of Bengal. He was soon thereafter deposed by the latter-named monarch; fled to Arracan, and there perished miserably. When visited by Bishop Heber, the ruins of the palace were in comparatively good preservation; subsequently, however, their materials were utilised in the construction of the magnificent palace of Moorshedabad.

Two incidents now occurred, each characteristic in its way. A

8. In subsequent years large numbers of them were converted to Christianity; colonies established by them in Cachar and Assam.

soldier having clandestinely obtained bazaar spirit, was thereby rendered drunk and desperate; boasting of his courageous deeds, he was challenged to "take a header" into the Ganges. He did so, and appeared no more. The other was the infliction of one hundred lashes on the back of a hardened old offender, simply as punishment, for none of those who knew the man expected that it would have any deterrent effect in the future.

Entering the Bhauguruttee branch of the Ganges, our fleet was soon at Berhampore,[9] whence I had started up the river little more than two years previous. Again, but now as one of a body of officers, I partook of hospitality shown to the whole regiment by General Raper. A breakfast given at the palace of the *Nawab*;[10] excursions by land and river, presentation to His Highness, permission to visit different parts of his palace, including jewel-room and its contents, were so many items connected with ovation given to us as representatives of a distinguished regiment. All this was wound up by dinner at the house of the General, followed by a "Reception," during which I had the pleasure of again meeting some "old "friends.

Among the guests at that Reception was "the Khasjeewalla of Gwalior," implicated, as we have seen, in the disturbances that led to the recent campaign in that State. For a time he was interned at Agra, but latterly had been "at large," under surveillance of our host; his demeanour towards those by whom the victory at Punniar was gained, by no means agreeable; but under the circumstances anything else could hardly have been looked for.

9. In 1757 a stately range of two-storied barracks for "European" troops were erected at a cost of £302,278, the *rupee* then worth 2s. In 1834 they were abandoned on account of high rates of sickness and mortality among their occupants; average admission rate of 13 years per 1,000 strength, admissions 2,196, deaths 82. Of certain endemic diseases treated the rates of deaths to admissions were:—fever, 1 in 21; dysentery, 1 in 10; hepatitis, 1 in 9.

10. Then sixteen years of age. His grandfather, Jaffer Ali, Wuzzeer of Suraj ood Dowlah, *Nawab* of Bengal, a member of the Imperial family of Delhi, whom Lord Clive defeated at Plassee in 1757. It is related that on that occasion Jaffer Ali bribed a number of Suraj ood Dowlah's troops; with them he deserted his chief and went over to the English side. Subsequently the *Nawab* was assassinated, and Jaffer Ali raised to a position he had no right to claim. Thenceforward the *Nawab* of Moorshedabad was an "ally" of the British Government.

Resuming our journey, we soon arrived at and glided past the village of Plassee,[11] but the actual field so named had long since been swept away by the river by which we were being carried along. At Kulnah,[12] indications of flow and reflux of the tide were evident. There we met the fleet of boats, similar to our own, by which the 10th Regiment was being conveyed inland. Mutual salutations passed between us, but little at the time thought I of close association subsequently in store for me in relation to it. A short distance more, and we passed the village of Balaghurree, its inhabitants, those and their descendants, who, having been left by their relatives to die by the side of the river, were rescued through the good offices of missionaries.

We were nearing the end of this river journey. In quick succession our fleet glided past the important native towns of Bandel, noted on account of its Roman Catholic convent; Hooghly, for its college; and Chinsurah, already mentioned. Now we were off Chandernagore, on the battlements of which waved the tricolour. In 1757 that little settlement was captured from the French by Clive, aided by Admiral Watson, who, for the attack, brought thither his frigate carrying seventy-four guns—a feat not now possible because of the silting up of the river. The place was shortly afterwards restored to the French, to again fall to the British during the Revolutionary War, and finally to be ceded to them in accordance with the Peace Treaty of 1816.

We are well within the influence of the tide. As it recedes we are borne towards Calcutta. A forest of masts becomes more and more dense; tall chimneys on either bank tell of factories; the clang of hammers, of ship-building yards; the odour of tar, that we are nearing our port; and great is the surprise with which our north-country servants and followers look upon the unwonted sight. We pass the Armenian Ghat. It' is an open space, on which various funeral pyres blaze and smoke; vultures and adjutant-birds are waiting for such human remains as may be left: the scene most unpleasant to look at. For many years past that which

11. Plassee. From Palasa, "*dâk* tree," or *Butea frondosa*.
12. Kulnah is 164 miles from the Sandheads.

has just been alluded to has ceased to exist, a crematorium having taken its place. We arrive at Calcutta; the regiment lands, and marches into Fort William.

Preparations for departure proceeded rapidly, and with a will. Hospitality to the regiment and attentions in other ways were shown by some of the higher officials. At Government House some of us had an opportunity of being present at the dinners and balls, for which it was then, as since, well and favourably known; also at parties given by the Chief Justice Sir Lawrence Peel, in the spacious house occupied by him at Garden Reach.

The issue to men and officers of the Bronze Star respectively for Punniar and Maharajpore took place, but without pomp and circumstance such as most properly at the present time are observed on similar occasions. Being informed that the stars in question, composed of metal of Mahratta cannon that had wrought heavy injury to our regiments, were in readiness, in company with my friend Maude,[13] I drove to the Mint, and there, from two heaps on the floor, of those decorations, selected one each, leaving both for the purpose of our respective names being engraved on them. A few days thereafter we returned, and having received from an *employé* of that establishment the much-prized decorations, we placed them in our pockets, and drove back to Fort William.

Soon thereafter,[14] the Headquarter portion of the regiment was on board the *Monarch,* and away from India homeward bound. Our ship, one of a class by which troops were wont in favoured instances to be conveyed between England and her great Eastern dependency: graceful to look at, roomy, well fitted up, sumptuously provided—veritable floating palaces. The comfort of the soldier, his wife and children, secured to an extent that under subsequent regulations became impossible. With regard to officers, "stoppages" for messing was on the scale already mentioned. I became entitled to "head money," as on the outward

---

13. Now, after an interval of fifty-two years, I still am proud to call him friend, Alas! since the above was written he has passed away.
14. January 19, 1845.

voyage, notwithstanding that I was in the performance of my ordinary duties with my own regiment.

Nine weeks of uneventful life passed, and our ship was at St. Helena. Very shortly thereafter, parties of us, arranged for the purpose, landed at James's Town, the population of which seemed to consist almost entirely of mulattoes of low type, physically and intellectually; the balance were of pure negro type. We learned, moreover, that slave ships with their human cargo on board were from time to time brought to the island by British ships of war, very harrowing details being given of the sufferings of the unfortunate captives on board. At the time of our visit the garrison of the island comprised the St. Helena regiment and a battery of artillery.

An excursion to Longwood proved to be a somewhat arduous undertaking—carriages rickety, horses like living skeletons, lame, and weak, the ascent steep, rugged. The six or seven miles to be traversed required several hours for completion of the task. At last we were at and within the barn-like, dilapidated building in which took place the closing life scenes of Napoleon; its surroundings a tangled mass of brambles and other shrubs. In the building itself his library room, then partly filled with hay; near it the stable, having stalls for six horses. In a pretty valley close by, under the shade of the then famous willow, was the open tomb whence the remains of the great Frenchman were removed in 1840 for transport to the banks of the Seine.

Continuing our voyage, an incident which happened during its further progress deserves record. While sailing under the influence of the trade winds, a sailor fell from aloft into the sea. Quickly were life-buoys slipped, the ship brought round, a boat lowered, while from top-gallant cross-trees an officer directed the crew towards the man struggling in mid ocean. Soon, from the bows of the boat one of its crew dived, for the drowning man had already begun to sink; a brief interval, and both rescuer and rescued were hauled on board. With no loss of time the boat was alongside and on board ship, the man restored to animation and life by means used to that end. Many years thereafter, meeting Mr. Cloete, who performed the gallant act, we talked over the incident and its surrounding circumstances.

Another month at sea, and the *Monarch* swings at anchor off Gravesend; the Buffs, absent from England since 1821, disembark;[15] the ordeal of the Custom House gone through; the march on foot begun, for as yet a railway had not been opened. Evening was far advanced when the regiment arrived at Chatham, where it was to be temporarily quartered. In accordance with the routine of that day, nothing whatever had been prepared in barracks for our men, save that doors were open, displaying bare walls, bed cots devoid of mattress or bedding; while for the officers, not even quarters had been assigned; they were expected to look after themselves.

Night had far advanced before duty rendered necessary by such a state of things was so far complete as to allow of our going in search of hotels in which to spend the few hours that remained till daylight. It was not till two o' clock in the morning that we had "dinner, "in course of which various allusions were made to the "hospitality" accorded to us as a body on the occasion of our return, as contrasted with what we had experienced in India. Two days had to elapse before the regimental baggage arrived, though the distance over which it had to be conveyed was no more than ten miles; nor was it till then that straw for the men's cots was issued by the barrack stores, and they initiated into the art of stuffing their allotted quantities into their *palliasses.* This was the beginning of our Home Service.

---

15. On April 29, 1845.

CHAPTER 6

1845-1846. Home Service

Time-expired and some other classes of men not conducive to regimental efficiency being discharged, soldiers and officers "set up" in respect to kits and equipments, the order to proceed to Chichester was received with acclamation, for in those days the reputation accorded to Chatham as a station was by no means flattering. At the end of May the Buffs marched merrily away; that is, marched on foot, for railway communication had not yet connected Chatham with the outside world. A few miles got over, and we were at Blue Bell Hill, the ascent of which revealed to us in great variety and luxuriance forest, flowers, and grass-covered patches; the summit reached, an extensive view of the lovely vale of Kent stretched away beneath us, and in our near vicinity the cromlech called "Kittscotty House" [1] attracted the notice of those among us who were of antiquarian tastes.

At Maidstone the regiment had its first experience of transit by rail The art of "training" and detraining troops had not yet been learnt; hence delay such as would now be culpable was unavoidable before soldiers and their baggage were in their places, and a start made. The line being open only to Redhill, all had there to alight, the short journey to Reigate being performed on foot. Arrived at that pretty town, we had our initiation into the

---

1. It is related that in A.D. 455 a battle took place near this spot between the Saxons under Hengist and Horsa, and the Britons under Vertimer, the latter being victorious; that among the killed were Horsa, the Saxon, and Catigern, the brother of Vertimer. One account relates that the *cromlech* alluded to is that of Catigern, Horsa having been killed at Horsted near Rochester.

system of billeting, the officers being "told off" to the principal hotel, the comforts of which made us speedily forget whatever disagreeables had attended the proceedings of the day.

Continuing our journey, we arrived in succession at Petworth and Horsham, at each of which towns we similarly enjoyed our billets; thence to Chichester. The approach of a country gentleman to our Commanding Officer attracted our attention; the "halt" was sounded; the word passed on that, on hospitality intent, he had provided "refreshments "for all of us. His kind attention was highly appreciated, acknowledgments expressed, he himself invited to dinner with the officers at our new destination; then the march resumed, the Buffs marching into quarters at Chichester on the fourth day of their very pleasant journey.

Compared and contrasted with a march in India, that now over presented some striking points of difference, not the least of which were the absence of *hackeries*, bullocks, camels, elephants, and that heterogeneous collection of "followers" comprised under the name of "the bazaar." Instead of tents and camp fare we had comfortable if expensive entertainment at hotels, while our daily line of route lay through rich, varied, and beautiful English scenery. But some of our party looked back with fond remembrances to the freedom and feeling of exhilaration attending the early morning march in India, dusty roads and sundry other drawbacks notwithstanding.

The huts, literally *"baraques,"* assigned to us were old, dating from the Peninsular War. From the restoration of peace they had been left unoccupied until quite recently, when they were utilised in the first instance for the temporary reception of men enlisted to form a new 44th Regiment, and subsequently by the 55th on its return from China. The officer[2] who held the position of Barrack-master boasted of a very honourable military "record," he having been, if not the very first, among the first to mount the breach at Badajos; yet, like many others of his day, he had been thrown on half-pay at the conclusion of the war, and so deprived of the chance of rising in the service.

2. Lieutenant Graham.

From the residents of the cathedral city and its neighbourhood our officers received much civility and hospitality. The cathedral, used as a stable in the days of Cromwell, but long since "restored," was often visited, the circumstance that it had been transported from Selsey to its present site adding to it many points of historical interest. But to some among us Chichester had the great disadvantage of not yet being in direct communication by railway with London, the journey to and from the metropolis having to be performed by coach. A Bill had then only recently been passed authorizing such a railway.

An event occurred while we occupied those huts which marked in its way a stage in the advance of comfort and wellbeing of the soldier. Hitherto his "regulation" daily meals were only two; namely, breakfast at 8 a.m., dinner at 1 p.m.—an interval of nineteen hours being thus left during which he had to be without food, unless he happened to have spare money wherewith to supply himself at the regimental canteen or public-house in town. The obvious drawbacks of such a state of things had long been subject of representation, but hitherto unsuccessfully. Now, however, in 1845, authority was issued granting the issue to the men of a tea meal at 4 p.m. For a time the order was resented; that a soldier should condescend to tea was held to be against the natural order of things, and to mark effeminacy. Soon, however, the measure was appreciated by all, and drunkenness, at that time the bane of the soldier, underwent a remarkable decrease.

Winchester, to which we next proceeded, had "for ages" been looked upon as a favourite station by regiments. To some of us the many historical associations connected with that ancient city became so many sources of interest and objects of study. The commodious barracks, occupied by the Buffs and Scots Fusilier Guards stood upon the site of what had been a royal palace, and still earlier a castle. The city itself dates back to B.C. 800. The cathedral—to which our visits became very frequent—occupies a site whereon stood, during the years of Roman occupation, an altar to Apollo, and, in times still more ancient, one devoted to sun worship. Among other places of interest in and around the city were the buildings to which more particularly are referred the legendary stories of Saint Swithin of rainy fame; the ancient hospital of St. Cross, at which travellers might claim a dole of bread and beer; the world-famous school and college, both founded by William of Wykeham, A.D. 1324-1404.

Among favourite walks was that to "the Labyrinth," on the summit of St. Catherine's Hill; several alongside the banks of the Itchin, sacred to the memory of Izaak Walton, and that to Twyford. In the churchyard of that place stood a remarkably fine specimen of a yew tree, such as, in times long gone by, were preserved in burial places, and so held in a manner sacred—for the purpose of supplying yeomen with long-bows, in the use of which weapon those of England so much excelled. The hill from which, in Cromwell's time, the city was bombarded was a favourite walk among us. So was the village of Horsely, some few miles distant; its church associated with the author of *The Christian Year,* the choir, consisting of various very ordinary musical instruments, including a violin and clarionet.

On a day late in January, 1846, the Buffs proceeded by rail to Portsmouth. Bitterly cold, wet and windy, was the weather; the streets of that great naval port in some places inundated by the tide, so that progress along them was by no means pleasant. By the floating steam bridge the harbour was crossed, our regiment divided so as to occupy barracks at Forton and Haslar respectively. With the companies proceeding to the latter place I was detailed for duty. The quarters consisted of huts, the one assigned to me so situated as to afford from its window a near view of Spithead, and of the magnificent and graceful sailing men-of-war vessels anchored there or manoeuvring in the Solent.

An early opportunity was taken to visit the great Naval Hospital, near to which my temporary residence was situated; and although in these notes professional recollections are for the most part avoided, one of the results of that visit was sufficiently interesting to be made an exception to that rule.

On a portion of the adjoining grounds, and set apart for the purpose, a considerable number of mentally afflicted patients, together with their attendants or keepers—their costumes in every respect similar to those worn by the patients—were engaged with apparent heartiness in what was a "rollicking "dance, to the notes of several violins, the performers on which were presumably patients and attendants.

In the treatment of the patients all coercive measures were absent; free association among them was permitted from time to time, as we had seen; such of them as desired to work or labour were given every opportunity of doing so, and for the special benefit of those who desired to follow—in imagination—their seafaring life, a lake with its fleet of boats was provided. Such were some of the measures adopted in respect to this class of patients in 1846. The *Victory* and other "sights" connected with the great naval port were visited; but in respect to these it appears unnecessary to enter into details, except that all associations on board relating to England's naval hero were duly venerated.

Without previous warning news circulated that the Sikhs, in great force, had crossed the Sutlej, and thus invaded British territory. Then quickly followed intelligence that four severely contested battles against them had been fought, their forces defeated, Lahore occupied; Dhuleep Singh, a child, brought by his mother, the Maharanee, to the camp of Lord Hardinge, the Governor-General, by whom his "submission" was accepted.

In those battles many officers fell, with whom, collectively or individually, we had but recently, as already mentioned, been most pleasantly associated, and whose fate we now mourned. As fuller details became known, it appeared that on December 12, 1845, the Sikh armies, under the command of Lai Singh, crossed the Sutlej, and by the 16th had strongly fortified a position taken up by them on the left bank of that river. On the 13th the forces under Sir Hugh Gough attacked and drove them from their position at Moodkee.

Following them to Ferozeshuhur, at which place they had meanwhile entrenched themselves, he renewed his attack upon them on the 21st, the terrible battle which was to ensue continuing during that and two following days,—the issue, for some time uncertain, ultimately being in favour of our troops. There it was that the 62nd, with whom but lately we had been happy at Dinapore, having begun its advance against those entrenchments with twenty-three officers, lost seventeen of that number—eight killed on the field and nine wounded. But still another position, and it at Aliwal, was taken up by the retreating Sikhs, where, on January 28, 1846, they were attacked by the forces under Sir Harry Smith.

There the 16th Lancers performed the gallant deed of charging through a *ghola* (or mass) of Sikhs, their substitute for a square; then repeated the charge, destroying the enemy thus rode down. In the performance of that heroic feat the regiment lost upwards of one hundred men killed and wounded—that is, nearly one-third of their effective strength. On February 10 the Sikhs were defeated, their forces destroyed up at Sobraon, though at very heavy cost in killed and wounded to the British.

On that occasion the 50th lost in killed and wounded twelve officers, nearly all of whom were personal acquaintances, more or less intimate of my own, and in addition 227 men. The 10th Foot, with which I was destined to be subsequently associated, had in killed and wounded three officers, three non-commissioned officers, and 127 rank and file. Other regiments engaged suffered heavily, for the Sikhs contended for their nationality and class interests. The facts related give significance to the intentions of Lord Ellenborough expressed in Gwalior, to lead the troops thither direct upon the Punjab frontier. That plan was disallowed, and so two years were given to the Sikh leaders wherein to complete their arrangements for taking the offensive.

Orders from the Horse Guards directed that three infantry regiments—namely, the 8th, 24th, and 32nd—should proceed to India without delay. No less than six weeks elapsed, however, before they sailed, the circumstance itself illustrating the state of unreadiness for emergencies which then existed. The three regiments named were destined to take their parts in arduous service in India, the first at Mooltan, the second at Chilianwalla, the third at Lucknow.

The establishment of what was to be called our "Experimental Squadron" at this time was justly looked upon as an event of great importance. The fleet so designated consisted for the most part of sailing ships of war, but comprised also several steam vessels, propelled by paddles, the whole providing for spectators an unusual and magnificent sight as they lay anchored at Spithead.[3] Between the lines passed the Royal yacht, having on board Her Majesty the Queen. From the sides of each successive ship thundered salutes; from their decks rose strains of the National Anthem; from their yards, manned for the occasion, came hearty cheers of loyalty. A brief interval succeeded; then simultaneously, as if by combined movement, dropped the huge white sails; these gradually filled to the breeze; away glided the fleet, followed by hundreds of yachts, boats, and craft of all sorts. About this time also the then strange sight was for the first time witnessed of a war ship, the *Rattler,* sliding, as it were, out of Portsmouth Harbour, destitute of sail or paddle, the first of her kind propelled by the Archimedean screw.

The arrival at Spithead of the Russian war-ship *Prince of Warsaw,* having on board the Grand Duke Constantine, escorted by two other vessels, was to Portsmouth an event of interest and political importance. The officers of the Imperial frigate were entertained at dinner by those of the Buffs: an attention much appreciated by them. Next day a party of us were most civilly received on board their ship; in the course of that visit the circumstance made clear that our hosts were well acquainted with the English language, as also with insular manners and customs.

But great was the contrast between conditions on board and those of the "Experimental Squadron." The Russian sailors untidy and slovenly in appearance, the terms of their service severe, inasmuch as after a period of twenty years in the navy or army the reward to which they had to look forward was—emancipation; for as yet they were serfs. According to their own accounts, the period of obligatory service by officers was twenty-one

3. July 15—under command of Sir Hyde Parker.

years. Leave of absence, if exceeding a total of one year during that period, had to be made up by them; and if on any occasion absent from their ships or regiments for more than four days, their pay for that time is withheld from them. We congratulated ourselves that our position was in those respects more fortunate than theirs.

About the same time Ibrahim Pasha came among us. The circumstance that the comfort or otherwise of travellers across the desert between Cairo and Suez depended much on measures directed by the Viceroy of Egypt, added to other considerations, no doubt moved Admiralty and Horse Guards to order that every attention should be shown to His Highness. Among other displays for his gratification the troops in garrison were paraded on Southsea Common.

As he rode along the line, the impression produced by his appearance and style was by no means favourable; about fifty years of age, bloated in aspect, cruel and relentless in expression, he looked in these respects a true descendant of his father, Mehemet Ali.

In quarters at Portsmouth were the 13th Light Infantry, then recently returned from India, their honours thick upon them, as "The Illustrious Garrison." The 74th, reconverted into Highlanders, paraded for the first time in their newly-acquired uniform. In those regiments and in the Buffs there was a large leaven of old soldiers who had not risen beyond the ranks; the majority of the non-commissioned officers were men whose locks were grey, some with sons serving as soldiers; recruits were .relatively few in number; barrack-room courts-martial in full operation; crime, at least that officially brought forward, comparatively rare, though what in reality is quite another thing. That the regiments so constituted were capable of the most arduous service was proved by that of the Buffs in Gwalior, the 13th in Afghanistan.

The receipt from the War Office of a letter containing an offer of promotion conditional on proceeding to the West Coast of Africa, though a surprise, was not altogether an agreeable one, for hitherto the usual designation of that part of the world had been "The White Man's Grave." Official reports[4] regarding it referred to no later date than 1825; but this is the result of reference to them:—

In February of that year a party of white soldiers, 105 strong, arrived at the Isles de Loss, near Sierra Leone; at the end of eighteen months fifty-four of their number were dead by fever, eight by other diseases, twenty-one invalided back to England, twenty remained on those islands, scarcely any of them fit for duty. Then followed a table by which, at the Gambia, the annual mortality of white men was shown to have been at the rate of 1,500 per 1,000 average strength. On the other hand, the proffered promotion would advance me over one hundred and forty of my seniors; increased pay[5] would be an immediate advantage, and, in the event of survival, increased departmental position. The upshot of thought given to the subject was that, in the expression common to the time, I volunteered for the West Coast.

With regret and sorrow I ceased[6] to be a member of the distinguished old [7] regiment, with the traditions and history of which, like all its other members, I had become familiar. I had, moreover, formed friendships [8] such as subsequent experience taught me existed only between regimental officers during early life. The kindly expressions addressed to me by the Commanding Officer on the occasion of the farewell dinner, to which I was invited, impressed me in a manner not to be forgotten, and are here alluded to as indicating the relations then existing between medical and battalion officers.

No regular line of communication existed between England

4. Statistical Reports by Major Tulloch.

5. Regimental pay, 7s. 6d. per day; mess and band subscriptions deducted from it.

6. July 10, 1846, Staff-Surgeon, 2nd class.

7. Dating back to A.D. 1572, when, under Elizabeth, the regiment was formed out of the Trained Bands of London, its uniforms of Buff leather, whence its name, now a proud title.

8. Now, alas! while these notes are being transcribed, only one remains; namely, General Sir Frederick Francis Maude, G.C.B. Only lately did my other great friend, Deputy Surgeon-General Bostock, C.B., Q.H.S., die. While the notes are under revision, Maude has passed away.

and the West Coast of Africa; consequently, when orders to embark were received, passage had to be negotiated for through the medium of a ship's broker, and so advantage taken of trading brigs or other small craft proceeding, at irregular times, on voyages thither, either from the Thames or Mersey. Several months elapsed before transport was obtained, and, meanwhile, time was spent in visiting places interesting in themselves or by reason of past associations.

At this time public attention became aroused to a state of ferment, ostensibly because of the death of a soldier of the 7th Hussars at Hounslow, after having been flogged to the extent of 150 lashes, in pursuance of a sentence to that effect by court-martial, for having violently and dangerously assaulted a non-commissioned officer of his regiment. Medical opinion differed *in toto* as to whether the death was, or was not, the effect of the corporal punishment. But the case was taken up and energetically debated, not only at public meetings convened for the purpose, but also in both Houses of Parliament.

Whatever may have been its intrinsic merits, the case in question undoubtedly led to the introduction of a Bill, the outcome of which was that the maximum number of lashes to be inflicted was thenceforward reduced to fifty. Instead of "unlimited" service as heretofore, the period of a soldier's engagement was reduced to ten years; and so, it was hoped, encouragement held out for a better class of recruits to join the ranks; desertion would be diminished, and the general efficiency of the service increased.

In September, 1846, the death of Thomas Clarkson, at the age of eighty-six, recalled attention to the subjects of slavery and the slave trade, against both of which, for many years, his energies had been directed. It was in 1720 that English opinion was first drawn to the horrors incidental to that traffic. In 1787, by the efforts of Clarkson and Granville Sharp, a Society for total abolition of the system was formed. In the following year a Committee of the House of Commons was appointed to inquire into the entire system; but not for a considerable time could the objects of that Society be carried out, or members of influence be induced to take interest in the Anti-Slavery Association and its work.

Suddenly, and as if through an accidental occurrence, public opinion was aroused; that accident, the seizure in the streets of London of an escaped slave, named Somerset—his late master, the captor. In 1792, Wilberforce carried a Bill for the gradual abolition of the slave trade. In 1805 the importation of slaves into British Colonies, recently taken from Holland, was prohibited; a Bill carried, by which such traffic after 1808 was declared illegal. In 1811 it was declared to be felony; in 1824 it was made piracy. In 1837, made punishable by transportation for life. In 1838, complete emancipation of slaves throughout all British possessions took place. We were soon to see the results of those measures in what had once been one of slavery's most active spheres.

CHAPTER 7

1847-1848. Coast of Guinea—
Barbados—England

Cold, misty, and raw was the day in the first week of January, 1847, when, at Gravesend, a small party, of which I was one, embarked on the brig *Emily*, bound to Cape Coast Castle. Still more miserable the four following days and nights, during which the little vessel remained at anchor, a thick dark fog enveloping us; horns and gongs sounding at intervals, to avert a collision, if possible. At last the pall lifted, and we were on our way. My fellow-passengers, four in number, were three junior officers of the 1st West India Regiment, and the wife of one of them. The ship had a burthen of only 130 tons; no separate cabins, no accommodation suitable for officers, and none whatever for a lady. Around the *cuddy*, as the "saloon" was called, a series of bunks were arranged; one of these was told off to each of us, ingress being attained either feet or head foremost, according to individual fancy and agility.

Every possible consideration was shown by all on board to the lady, whose sorry plight we all commiserated; hers was indeed a sad example of the discomforts to which a subaltern's wife was exposed. Our prospects so far were by no means happy, for the circumstance became increasingly plain that only "black sheep" were considered to be sent to "the Coast"; many years had to elapse before Africa was to spring into fashion. Fifty-two days at sea—for steam communication with the West Coast was a thing of the, future—and then the headland of Grand Drewin came in sight. That point sighted, our little ship glided along the coast, carried southward by the oceanic current at the rate of three knots an hour or thereabouts.

Arrived in the roads of Elmina, at the time a Dutch settlement, we disembarked by means of small canoes, made by hollowing out a branch of the *bombax* or silk cotton tree, each canoe "manned" by three black boys, the eldest of whom did not apparently exceed twelve years of age. We made direct for the house of Mr. Bartels, not that we had an introduction to that well-known gentleman, but for the double reason that "everybody "did so, and that Elmina boasted neither of hotel nor other public place to which new arrivals could resort. The hospitable gentleman on whom we had thus thrown ourselves showed us every kindness. Next day means of conveyance to our destination were provided for us. Mine consisted of a long narrow basket, carried on the heads of two strong Africans, one at either end. In that way we travelled over some miles of roadless ground; in others along the sea beach left dry by the receded tide, and so arrived at Cape Coast Castle, the capital of our settlements on the Coast of Guinea.[1]

The fortress had in its day been used for many purposes, from the time when in 1610 it was erected by the Portuguese, and by them made use of as a slave hold, down to the present (1847). Captured by the Dutch from its original possessors in 1643, it was taken from the latter by Admiral Holmes in 1661; recaptured by the Dutch fleet under De Ruyter in 1665, but the same year ceded to England. In 1757 it was attacked unsuccessfully by the French, since which it has remained free from the din of war, although from time to time conflicts have occurred between the native tribes occupying the neighbouring districts. In 1672 the first African Company received a charter from Charles II. From

1. When the first Europeans trading between Benin and Palmas asked where the gold and produce offered them for sale came from, the natives answered, "From Jenné" (on the Niger, near Timbuctoo). Her name was thus given to the Gulf of Guinea, and, indirectly, to the English coin, the guinea. *(Timbuctoo the Mysterious,* by Felix Dubois, p. 172.)"

that date till 1844 the fort continued in the possession of that Company and its successors; in the year named it came directly under the administration of the Colonial Office, as a dependency of Sierra Leone.

At the time of our sojourn there, Cape Coast Castle was occupied by a portion of a West India regiment by officers belonging thereto, and to military departments; by the Governor, also by the "mixed court," by which law or justice, or both, were administered. A school for African children, the apartment being used for Divine service on Sundays, was in close proximity to the billiard-room. An annexe of the fort was utilised as a prison for the worst class of malefactors, and the native police in charge of them, the prisoners being engaged in chain gangs by day, working on roads and public works within the settlement. Since the days of slavery, what had been "*barracoons*" for captives have been transformed into water tanks for the supply abundantly provided by the rainy season.

The inhabitants of the territory around Cape Coast Castle and of the Gold Coast generally are in the mass known as Fantees. Originally dwellers in the regions beyond the river Prah, they were forced to cross it, and driven to the coast line by the people now called Ashantees, who took possession of and gave their name to the country so conquered. Although under protection of the British Government, the Fantee chiefs (in 1847) pay tribute to the Ashantee king, who still assumes suzerainty over them. That suzerainty, since 1826, has been maintained without right on their part, the Ashantees having in that year been defeated at Doodwa, near Accra, by a Fantee force, led by British officers. In the same year, however, though earlier in it, a small force,[2] under Sir Charles Macarthy, was disastrously beaten by the Ashantees.

That officer, rather than fall alive into the hands of his enemies, is said to have shot himself; they to have devoured his heart, in the belief that by that act of cannibalism they might

2. Mr. Barnes, with whom I was acquainted in 1847, had been with that force in 1826.

become endowed with the high attributes which they admired in him.

A noticeable characteristic of the people was the total absence among them of ceremony, rite, or other observance pertaining to religious worship. That certain phases of superstitious impressions existed among them was evident by their belief in "lucky" and "unlucky" days. Neither a fisherman nor bushman would proceed on their avocations on a Friday, as it was by them devoted to their "Fetish." [3] Although caste as understood in India is unknown among Fantees, the existence of *septs* or families approaches in some respects the social and religious divisions of the Hindoos. Each Fantee *sept* is distinguished by its special badge or armorial bearing, taken usually from some wild animal of the forest, as among Scottish Highlanders and other civilized nations, ancient and modern.

Ten years had nearly elapsed since slavery on the Gold Coast, as in all other British dominions, was abolished. In all but name conditions remained unchanged; former domestic slaves, now called servants, remained with their former owners, by whom they were housed, clothed, and fed as heretofore. It was related that when, in 1838,[4] emancipation was proclaimed, the negroes here appealed against being "sent away," on the plea that they and their children had ever been cared for; that as freed men and women they were without country to return to, or means of earning their living, save with their old masters and mistresses. Their appeal was listened to, and now (1847), when asked jokingly, rather than in earnest, to whom do they belong, they answer proudly that they are "slave" of, say Mrs. Jackson, Mr. Barnes, Mr. Hutton, and so on, all highly respected residents of Cape Coast.

A "slave" girl of the class alluded to having died, ceremonies, elaborate in kind, took place over her body. Placed in a sitting posture, and so supported in a corner of a room, it was enveloped in a shroud of costly damask; the feet rested upon a cushion similarly covered; neck and arms decorated with heavy orna-

---

3. From the Portuguese *Fetisso,* a spell, or charm.
4. From August 1, 1838, slaves became free.

ments of solid gold; the body embellished by more or less artistic designs composed of gold dust applied to some adhesive material. In the mouth was a twig of shrub; on an adjoining table a goodly supply of rum and tobacco.

On the floor of the room sat a crowd of female mourners, whose dirge was loud if not melodious. These ceremonies over, the dead, still covered with ornaments, was deposited in the grave prepared for it in the floor of the dwelling-house of the survivors; but, as stated to us, at the end of a year, the body would be "turned on its side to make it comfortable," and then the golden ornaments removed.

Two months had elapsed since our arrival, and impressions of the place were noted after this manner:—

At the end of February, temperature in the shade between the moderate extremes of 84^0 F. and 86° F.; sky clear and cloudless, sea breeze recurring each morning, and continuing during the hours of daylight. Behind, and from close proximity to the town, the "bush" or dense forest begins; two inconsiderable hills, each surmounted by a "fort," dominate us. Some few roads or pathways extend in various directions inland and along the beach side to the Salt Pond, their borders lined with cacti and with flowering shrubs,[5] the occurrence of reptiles of various kinds, and creeping things innumerable, adding to our walks of interest and excitement in giving the former chase.

Among the forest trees a species of *bombax* was a striking object, its branches so thickly covered with nests of the tailor-bird *(Ploceus)* that they touched each other, and looked not unlike a series of gigantic honeycombs. The absence of the bamboo was noted with surprise, considering the latitude of the locality. Nor was any cultivated field to be seen, the explanation being that each year small patches of the bush are cut down, the ground cleared, crops sown or planted, and once gathered in the "field" is quick

5. *Thespesia*, acacias, including the sensitive plant, *abrus, convolvuli*, palms, wild figs, tamarind, etc.

ly restored to its original wild state till again required for agricultural purposes. Birds and butterflies, some of both highly coloured, dashed through or fluttered among, the herbage, but no voice of song properly so called as yet came from the former.

With the advent of the tornado season, the face of nature underwent a sudden change. From the south-east came rapidly a mass of dense black cloud. As it seemed arrested overhead, it assumed the form of an arch; from its concavity forked lightning flashed, then heavy thunder rolled. The previous stillness gave place to a rush of wind at hurricane speed, followed by such a downfall of rain as we had never previously seen, even in India. A few repetitions of these, and the rainy season was upon us. Then suddenly cultivation was begun in places previously covered by bush; crops of Indian corn, yams *(Convolvulus Batatas)*, ground-nuts *(Aradtis hypogea)*, and the castor-oil plant sprang up with a rapidity truly astonishing.

With the first regular downpour of rain came a serious change in health of our small party within the fort, also of the few settlers whose places of business were in the town immediately outside; and for a few succeeding months we were destined to realize the true significance of a sickly season on the Coast of Guinea. Fever in one or other of its local forms made its appearance, affecting the older residents in that of ague, while the newly arrived were attacked by the more violent form, called at the time their "seasoning," from which the chances of recovery were considerably less than those of death.

Of the three officers and the wife of one who had been my fellow-passengers, one of the former speedily succumbed. The other two, together with the lady, suffered severely, and made imperfect recoveries, while outside the fort conditions were no less serious. The blanks so made in our numbers were sadly apparent, and yet the survivors from attacks, and those who had not been struck down, found in each successive death this rather ghastly consolation, that, as the *ratio* of mortality was "being made up," so did their chances of escape increase.

All this while the few of us who were capable of the exertion took our walk morning and evening when the weather permitted, our one promenade that towards "the Salt Pond." As we did so, the melancholy sight presented itself, of a small number of newly arrived missionaries[6] gloomily pursuing the same route, "waiting," as we were informed, "for their seasoning," before being sent inland to their respective stations. One after another was missed; it was announced that "he was down with his seasoning"; and then—the receipt of a black-edged envelope told the rest.

Meantime I retained my health to a degree that under the circumstances was remarkable. As a result of this happy exemption from sickness, various duties devolved upon me in addition to those within my proper sphere, among those extra responsibilities being professional work in the Colonial Hospital, and charge of the Commissariat Department for the troops—the latter altogether alien to my training or tastes. So conditions went on till July, a month which proved to be the most unhealthy and deadly of any throughout the year.

It was then that, night after night, I was the solitary member of "our mess" who took his place at table. I made, the acquaintance of, and speedily became on friendly terms with, some mice, whose place of residence was under the floor, but which freely communicated with the mess-room by numerous apertures, and was in other respects dilapidated; nor did it take long before some of the little animals acquired sufficient confidence to scramble up my leg and so on to the table, partake of dinner with myself, thus calling to my mind the story of the *Prisoner of Chillon*. With the month of August came improved health conditions, and for the four or five succeeding months all was cheerful in that particular and important respect.

Among those who succumbed during the sickly months was Captain Maclean, husband of the poetess, L. E. L.—Letitia Elizabeth Landon, who died at Cape Coast Castle in 1838, under circumstances of great mystery. It was hoped that among his papers would be found some containing his own account of

6. Of the Wesleyans.

the sad occurrence, but that hope was not realized. From careful inquiries, however, I was led to the belief that her death was due to natural causes, and to them alone. Now the body of the deceased husband was laid in the grave close to that of the wife,[7] and both rest under the pavement of the castle quadrangle. The story of the gifted lady interested some of our number, as incidents connected with her short life on the Coast were related by Mr. Hutton and others who had enjoyed her acquaintance.

The occurrence of the "healthy season" was hailed as such event could only be in a locality where every man had to run the gauntlet for life during four to five out of the twelve months which make up the year. Amusements of different kinds were instituted, short excursions taken in various directions along such roads or pathways as existed for purposes of communication along the coast and to places inland. In the absence of horses—for these most useful animals when brought to the coast rapidly pine away and die—our means of transport consisted, for the most part, of a chair so placed between two poles as to be thus carried by two or four Africans, according to the weight of the individual.

There were a few small light carriages, in some respects like a Bath chair, in others like a victoria, drawn by Africans, who, to judge by their antics and shouts as they raced against each other, must have enjoyed the work immensely. Picnics became "the order of the day"; Saints' days, birthdays, and holidays were most "religiously" kept, and for the most part very enthusiastically celebrated. On one of these occasions we visited what at one time had been a coffee plantation in the near vicinity, but then deserted; the buildings reduced to ruin, the coffee bushes choked by the ordinary bush, the natural impression being that the owner had fallen a victim to his "seasoning," that he had no successors on his estate;[8] or, if he had, that they had also succumbed.

---

7. Some account of L. E. L. is given in my separate book, *Life on the Gold Coast*. I consider that the cause of her death was disease of the heart, with which she was known to have been affected several years.
8. Still called "Napoleon."

Pursuits relating to natural history became so many sources of pleasant and intellectual occupation. Ornithology was especially interesting, combining as it did observation of birds in their natural haunts and conditions. A large number of specimens were shot, one portion being subsequently given to the Natural History Museum of Edinburgh, another to Sir William Jardine, by whom notes taken at the time were published.[9] A song bird *(Drymoica mentalis)* that fell to my gun was for the first time, I believe, given as an illustration in that brochure; another illustration being that of a large and handsome swallow named after me, *Hirundo Gordoni.*

On one occasion, while combining ornithological study and "sport," I had an unpleasant experience with one of several kinds of poisonous snakes that here abound, frequenting chiefly prickly herbage in immediate proximity to such roads and pathways as then existed, as also the sedgy tract of open ground near the Salt Pond, a little way westward of the settlement. While traversing that tract I came suddenly face to face with a large black cobra. One barrel of my fowling-piece had been already discharged. The remaining shot—a mixture of Nos. 6 and 9—was fired, more as a result of instinctive action than steady aim, by me, but with good effect.

The charge traversed the body of the reptile as if it were a bullet, so close was it to me; then its writhings were such that I came within them, not a little to my own horror. In the emergency my Fantee "boy" speedily dispatched it by means of the heavy stick he carried for the purpose of beating the bush. The skin—considerably over six feet long—ornamented the wall of my barrack-room while I remained on the coast. Puff-adders are numerous, and from their sluggish movements are easily killed. On one occasion I killed six partially-grown individuals during a morning's walk on the Salt Pond road.

When, as already stated, administration of British settlements on the Gold Coast was taken over by the Colonial Office, it was made immediately subordinate to that of Sierra Leone. The in-

9. Under the title of *Contributions to Ornithology.*

convenience of that arrangement was soon made manifest. The force with which the oceanic current runs southward along the coast is sufficient during some months of the year to prevent sailing brigs from beating up against it; and as at the time alluded to a regular line of steamers had not been introduced, the outcome of that state of things was the inconvenient necessity of letters and dispatches for the headquarters of the Government and Command being sent *via* England, several months becoming thus necessary before answers could be received.

Cape Coast Castle and its dependencies had a Governor and Colonial Secretary, both of whom were resident.. Justice was administered by a court presided over by a British official designated Judicial Assessor, assisted by selected native chiefs. Of them, "King Aggary," then upwards of eighty years of age, was the most prominent and distinguished. As a young man he had served on board a British man-of-war, in accordance with the custom of the time, and so, according to his own manner of expression, he "had learned sense."

For a long time past native rulers whose "kingdoms" adjoined British settlements along the Gold Coast had voluntarily placed themselves under protection of our flag, and thus in a manner become British subjects. Their several laws and customs were retained, with the exception of human sacrifice, a practice abandoned many years ago. Succession to rank and property descended through the female line; that is, the eldest son of the eldest daughter became heir-apparent. In the kingdom of Akim the sovereign is a female, the succession being also in the female line.

A visit to Accra occupied two days, and a similar time to return. The path along which I travelled—for no road existed—led for the most part through the bush close to the beach; at times it was by the beach itself, so that only when the tide was low was it practicable to proceed at all. At intervals the occurrence of rugged promontories and heaps of boulders rendered it by no means an easy undertaking to get over them. Arriving at the river Sekoom, its borders were lined by mangrove trees (*Rhizo-*

phora), the long tendril-like roots of which interlaced above the soft mud alternately covered and left exposed as the tide flows and ebbs.

In some places the trunks of those trees were covered within tide mark by a small species of oyster, and presented the additional peculiarity of a few small fish—the climbing perch (*Anabas scandens*) laboriously ascending to the height of a couple of feet or so from the water level, there "holding on" for a little, then dropping into the muddy river after basking in the sun. At Accra, three forts, belonging respectively to England, Holland, and Denmark, were in close proximity to each other: the first occupied by some twenty black soldiers and half a dozen native militiamen, the guns old and useless, the fortress itself dilapidated; the second nothing more than a trading store of the Governor; the third, the strongest of the three, but noted for its extreme unhealthiness. Subsequently we learned that it was completely destroyed by an earthquake.

Several of the forts that had belonged to the former African Company were abandoned some years previous to the present date (1848); among others that of Amelycha, or Apollonia, about seventy miles to windward of Cape Coast Castle. For a time matters in the district so called progressed very well under the rule of a humane and otherwise good native chief named Yansu Acko; but having died in 1830, he was succeeded by Quako Acko, a man of cruel and tyrannical disposition, who, although he continued to fly the British flag, gradually became less and less loyal, and finally withdrew allegiance altogether.

Meanwhile he was in a continual state of warfare with the States adjoining his own, extending his depredations to Asinee and Axim, respectively belonging to France and Holland. In 1835 his conduct had become so outrageous that a force from Cape Coast Castle was sent against him, and for his misconduct he was subjected to a fine of 300 ounces of gold dust. So little effect had this upon him, however, that in 1838 a second expedition was sent against him, and a further fine of 800 ounces inflicted upon him. From that time to the present he has persisted in annoying the adjoining States. Within his own "kingdom" his word was absolute, his great ambition apparently to surround his palace with festoons composed of skulls of enemies slain in battle or of captives butchered.

With increasing boldness as time went on, he destroyed several villages within Dutch territory, and carried away some of their inhabitants. He maltreated officers and men belonging to French and British ships, who landed at his capital for purposes of trade. Finally, when remonstrated with by the Governor of Cape Coast,[10] he insulted and otherwise maltreated the members of the embassy sent to him, certain of whom he retained as captives. The Governor took action against the recalcitrant chief. Orders were issued directing the formation of a contingent force, some thousands strong, to consist of men pertaining to vassal tribes.

A brig was chartered for the occasion; ammunition and stores of various kinds, including casks of fresh water, placed on board; for it was known that the scene of coming operations was destitute of that necessary element. Ammunition was issued to the "volunteer" contingent, to whom pay in advance was distributed. At this point the officer [11] named to command fell ill and speedily died of coast fever, and his place had to be taken by a lieutenant[12], of the 1st West India Regiment; the Commissariat officer [13] being non-effective from sickness, the duties pertaining to his office fell upon me in addition to my own.

The resources of the colony in respect to white men limited the number of those available for the present expedition to six only, the "regular "troops to no more than about half a company of the 1st West India Regiment. Four of us by ship;[14] two accompanied the levies proceeding by land, their forces increasing as they advanced. Arrived off Dixcove, we landed at that place,

---

10. Commander, afterwards Sir W. Winniett, R.N. He died on the Coast.
11. Captain Losack.
12. Lieutenant Bingham. He lost his health during the expedition, and shortly thereafter died in England.
13. C. Swaine.
14. The brig *Governor Maclean*.

to witness the native ceremony, and excitement attending thereon, of "burying the peace-drum." The unusual noise and tumult connected with the ordeal seem to have attracted the notice of wild denizens of the adjoining forest, one of which, a baboon of large size, "assisted "with his presence on the occasion; he was declared to be "the great Fetish"; his advent to be a happy augury for the undertaking before us.

Our next point was Axim, at that time Dutch, but now British. There we landed; there the entire force at our disposal assembled, and arrangements were completed to enter hostile territory. The small party of whites was accommodated within the fort, the native forces bivouacking in and around the town,— the town consisting chiefly of sheds or huts composed of palm branches inartistically tied together. In the open space or market place in its centre stood a pole to which were fixed portions of human skeletons, remains of freebooters from Apollonia, who having been caught were "disposed of" according to African fashion. In the vicinity roads were non-existent; some rugged pathways were all the thoroughfares with which the place was provided.

Between Axim and the river Encobra stretched a sea beach two miles in extent, broken at intervals by irregular masses and boulders of primitive rocks; beyond it to a similar distance a belt of impenetrable forest, pathways through which, formerly existing, had for some years past become obliterated. Through that tract of bush we had to make a way, not only for ourselves, but also for our "forces." Armed with an axe and long knife such as bush men in this part of Africa use, we cut a path for ourselves to the summit of a promontory from which it was practicable to take bearings for further progress. eanwhile, and all through the following night, large numbers of men were busy clearing a road by which the mass of our contingent could advance.

At daybreak our strange body of irregulars was mustered, and what a sight it presented! War dresses, wild in character, grotesque in aspect; umbrellas of many colours, carried over particular chiefs; uncouth gesticulations in the performance of war dances; strange sounds from drums, horns, trumpets, and other "musical" instruments, the chief ornaments on which were jaw-bones and other fragments of human mortality, combined to impress us with the aspect of savagery so presented. At the head of one of the "companies," and in command, was a lady, who thus asserted her hereditary position as chief of her tribe.

In the early hours of a day in the first week of April (1848), our "army "began its march towards the left bank of the Enco-bra. By previous arrangement a number of canoes, sufficient to take the force across that river, were already outside the bar at its mouth, and these were quickly utilised for our purpose. A dense mass of natives crowded the opposite side of the river, its dimensions quickly increasing as others emerged from the bush. Our "artillery" consisted of two twelve-pounder rocket tubes, and two others of smaller calibre. In the absence of a "combat-ant" officer, I had been put in "command" of these, and having previously indulged in the necessary practice, was in a position to open fire upon the "enemy "as soon as the necessary order was given by the Governor, who was in supreme command.

A few missiles were discharged; a few lanes ploughed' among them, and then pell-mell the mass vanished in the forest. Having got across the river, we speedily reached an Apollonian village, deserted by its ordinary occupants, who in their haste had left behind their flocks and herds, both of which were quickly an-nexed by our "contingent." Continuing what proved to be an extremely fatiguing march along the sea beach,— often having to wade more than knee-deep in the rippling tide,—we passed on the border of the forest a succession of villages, from all of which their occupants had fled. Towards evening we reached a town of considerable size. Our day's march had been extremely exhausting, so that rest for the night was most welcome, espe-cially to us white men.

In the course of the succeeding night, such snatches of sleep as we obtained were several times interrupted by the beating of tom-toms, braying of trumpets, the rushing hither and thither of considerable portions of our army. Now it was an alarm of night attack by "the enemy"; then the noisy return of a foraging party, bearing with them as trophies the heads of two Apollonians, which they cast before the Governor as tokens of their prowess. Resuming our march early the following morning, we arrived at the river Abimoosoo, across which we were floated by means of canoes that had so far followed by sea, keeping just outside the line of breakers.

Shortly thereafter we were met by a messenger from "the king" against whom we were in progress; his office to express the desire of His Majesty to know with what object the Governor had brought an army into his country. The reply was a ball cartridge (according to the custom of the coast), together with a reply that if the king surrendered, then "a *palaver*" would be held, but not till then. Meantime we pressed on, and in the early part of the afternoon entered the capital of the king, to find it completely abandoned. Never before had I felt so "done up" and exhausted as now. I was, moreover, ill, and had every reason to believe that an attack of the much-dreaded fever of the coast was upon me.

As if to celebrate the entry of our "army" into the royal city, arrangements were speedily made by the native leaders to have a grand procession. When it did take place, no more wild and "savage" display could well be imagined than that presented by it. All around us were ghastly relics of death and murder. The palace garnished with festoons of human skulls, of which I counted one hundred and eighty after the greater part of such ornaments had been torn from their places and kicked about as playthings by our "soldiers." The avenue leading to the palace was formed by palm-trees growing at short distances from each other along either side of the roadway.

From time to time the king had disposed of a certain number of his enemies by living sepulture in a standing position; a cocoa nut placed on the head of each, the earth thrown in, and as in the progress of time the plume of palm grew higher and higher, each tree received the name of the particular enemy represented by it. At different points around, the larger trees were ornamented with various relics of humanity, skeleton hands and other fragments being nailed or otherwise attached to stems and branches.

During the few following days different portions of our contingent were variously employed. An expedition, led by two of our white associates,[15] started inland, with a view, if possible, to capture the fugitive king; another, consisting entirely of blacks, having started independently into the bush, returned in triumph, with "music," war dances, and much discordant noise, bearing with them gory heads of three Apollonians who had fallen into their power.

A third party of our people, having proceeded on an independent expedition, came upon two men who had been made prisoners by order of that chief, each of them laden with three sets of heavy irons, which they had worn continuously during the two previous years. The manacles were removed after much labour; but their unhappy bearers, when relieved of them, were unable to stand erect. So long had they been kept in a sitting posture by sheer weight of their fetters, that the joints had become accommodated to it. Shortly afterwards eighty-eight other prisoners were discovered, their fetters similarly removed, but they themselves fixed in the sitting posture to which they had for longer or shorter periods been borne down by iron manacles.

Everywhere around the town the bush was impenetrable, for all communication with neighbouring tribes had been cut off for some years past, the pathways thus become obliterated by the forest. Attempts to cut new ones were but partially successful. Meanwhile serious difficulties beset us in respect to water, for the lagoons and rivers within available distance being brackish, they quickly ceased to be resorted to. A few casks of fresh water from our chartered ship thrown overboard were washed ashore, their contents carefully distributed among ourselves; but the fact became very evident that this supply being extremely limited, our "occupation" of the town must be short indeed, whether the object of our expedition was obtained or not.

15. Messrs. Brodie Cruickshank and Frank Swanzy.

Most fortunate for us there was treason in the king's camp. By reason of his cruelty and tyranny, he had rendered himself hated by and hateful to his subjects. Now their opportunity had arrived. Three of their chiefs having tendered their submission, so far imitated certain civilized nations as to negotiate for the surrender of their king—their terms by no means exorbitant, namely one hundred ounces of gold dust, and a flag to them respectively. And so the bargain was closed.

A few more days passed, during which "palavers" of all sorts took place, and parties dispatched in various directions, though seemingly without result. Evening approaches; there is unusual tumult among our contingent. Discordant noises, emitted from drums, horns, and human mouths, announce the approach of large bodies of men; they are the former subjects of the king,[16] whom they carry manacled and give over to the British leader. We feel relieved by the prospect of speedy ending of our privations and fatigues; for of our number, four are prostrate by sickness. So long as our prisoner, savage as he is, continued out of sight, we did our best to follow him up relentlessly. Now that he is in our presence, bound hand and foot, an object of abject misery, big tears rolling down his coarse black face, some of us were unable to smother a shade of sympathy for the man, monster of cruelty as he was.

Of atrocities committed by him the record of two will here suffice. He caused his mother to be secured to a stake at low-water mark when the tide was out, her eyelids to be cut off, her face turned towards the sun,—so left until overwhelmed by the returning flood, and her sufferings put an end to. His pregnant sister he caused to be cut open while alive, that he might see the position in her womb of the unborn infant, then directed that according to native custom her body should be buried within the palace.

In the room under the floor of which the remains were interred, bearing upon them her golden ornaments, the captive king was placed under guard, and so remained during the fol-

16. Quako Acko by name.

lowing night. With the return of daylight it was seen that the floor had been opened by the guard, the remains exhumed, all ornaments wrenched therefrom; the body itself, considerably advanced in decay, offensive to sight and smell, thrown back into the still open grave. Thus the king had spent the night side by side as it were with the remains of his murdered sister, witness to the acts of savagery to which they were subjected.

Our object attained, the return march began at midnight; our prisoner, several of his wives, together with other members of his family, being under the charge of a strong guard. The four sick white men, unable to take their proper places in the ranks, were carried, country fashion, in the long baskets already described, our bearers being subjects of the king whom we were carrying away prisoner. Again the beach, left dry by the receded tide, was our highway, and along it our "brave" men proceeded.

How the sick fared is illustrated in my own experience. As the fierce tropical sun ascended in the heavens, the fever from which I suffered increased, headache was severe; fresh water there was none wherewith to moisten the parched mouth. In this plight, having by signs indicated my desire that my basket should be placed on the ground, I endeavoured to make my way to the ripples left by the recurring waves; but in so doing strength gave way, and I fell prostrate on the sand.

Immediately I found myself being gently lifted back to the basket by my carriers. One of them climbing a cocoa-nut tree that grew in our immediate vicinity, cut off a large specimen of its fruit, which was speedily opened by a companion beside me, its "milk" emptied over my face and given me to drink. At the time and often since I have thought gratefully of that act by the wild African, and have contrasted it with its counterpart met with among "civilized" peoples.

Arrived at Axim, and the necessary arrangements completed, we re-embarked on the little brig that had already done good service in connection with our expedition. The captive chief, or "king "as he was called, was speedily on board, under the care of a guard, the anchor raised. Wind and current favoured us, and so we quickly arrived off Cape Coast. In the early hours of morning we landed. Our prisoner was securely placed in a cell of that fortress. The populace of the native town, on hearing the news, were in great commotion; our friends, merchants and others, from whom we had parted a month before, were full of congratulations. Then followed invitations to dinner, picnics, and so forth, until the rainy season, already threatening, fairly broke upon us and put a stop to all.

Among other characteristic incidents related to us was that, as soon as our expedition had marched away, the women of Cape Coast, omitting the slight costume usually worn by them, went about their ordinary occupations in a state of nudity. One of the oldest of the foreign residents, astonished at the circumstance, inquired as to the reason for such an extraordinary proceeding; he received as answer from the perambulating statue so addressed the Fantee equivalent of "What does it matter? All the men have started for the war," much emphasis being given to the word "men."

The work of paying up and disbanding the contingent portion of the force was quickly carried out. In the former, gold dust was the currency employed, of which the equivalent value of three-halfpence was the daily rate given, no allowance being required for food. Years passed away, and then I learned that the wretched king, having lost his reason in his confinement, pined away, and died a drivelling idiot in his prison. One by one our party of white men engaged in this small but extremely trying piece of service dropped away, and for many years before the time when the present notes are transferred to these pages I have been the sole survivor. The expedition was mentioned approvingly in the *Times* some months after it had become a thing of the past. Medals and decorations for similar services in West Africa were then in the future.

Fifteen months on the Gold Coast; then came the welcome news that a ship with "reliefs" on board was sighted. Great was the excitement as we watched her gradual approach; great the zest with which their arrival was welcomed; hospitable the reception accorded to them; great the marks of kindness in various ways shown to us by residents. It was long since news had reached us from England, for regular mail communication did not exist. Papers now received were eagerly read, for they were filled with details illustrative of a threatening political aspect in various kingdoms of Europe.

Taught by experience how treacherous and dangerous was the climate of Cape Coast, I determined to proceed by the first ship to sail, irrespective of immediate destination, the chief object being "to get away." The arrival of the transport *Baretto Junior*, with reliefs of West Indian soldiers and African recruits for regiments in the West Indies, afforded me the desired opportunity. On 24th of May we embarked, the ship dropped with the current to Accra, and then sailed for Barbados.

Glad and thankful to have successfully run the gauntlet as it were against the climate of Guinea, the clear sea air, notwithstanding its temperature of 83^0 F., had its usual beneficial effect on health impaired on the Coast. The transport in which we sailed had on board three hundred Africans, of whom about one-half were soldiers, the remainder recruits, that is, captured slaves, selected from among those in the Adjudication Yard[17] at Sierra Leone, and duly "enlisted "into West India regiments. A good many of the soldiers were accompanied by their wives and children.

Among the "recruits" was a very strong athletic African named Kakungee, one of a cargo of slaves, the vessel conveying whom had recently been captured by a British man-of-war. A fellow-slave, but now "recruit," gave information of the violent and uncontrollable temper of Kakungee while on board the slave ship; that on two occasions he had suddenly attacked fellow-slaves, killing his victims before a rescue could be effected. With a view to guard against similar occurrences on board the *Baretto Junior*, he having speedily shown the violence of his disposition, he was secured to the deck by means of a cask—in one end of which

---

17. Slave-ships captured by British men-of-war were taken to Sierra Leone, their cargoes there transferred to the establishment so-named.

was a hole sufficiently large to let through his head, but not his shoulders—being put over him and cleated down. In that manner he was kept during the early part of our voyage, food and liquids given to him, but his hands prevented from being made use of for either purpose. His imploring requests to be relieved, and promises of good behaviour, led to his release, and being allowed to mix with his fellow-countrymen. Suddenly and without provocation he attacked a comrade. A Yorruba man of great physical strength came to the rescue; dealt the assailant such a blow that he reeled to leeward, and striking his head against a stanchion, lay insensible in the scupper. For nine days he remained in that condition, notwithstanding means used for his restoration; at the end of that time he died—a victim to his own incorrigible violence.

Twenty-nine days from Accra, our ship lay at anchor in Carlisle Bay, Barbados.[18] Proceeding on shore to make the usual official reports to the military authorities, we gained particulars in regard to the widespread revolutionary spirit through the nations of Europe; that in London serious demonstrations were threatened. Unhappily we also learned that an outbreak of yellow fever had occurred among the troops occupying barracks on the Savannah; that among victims of the disease were some medical officers. The upshot was that I was ordered on shore for duty. That afternoon I "took over" the barrack-room assigned to me, vacated very shortly before through death of its occupant. Disinfection and other means of modern sanitation were little if at all thought of in those days; nor, up to the present, close upon half a century since the event, has the malady extended to me.

The general aspect of Barbados is at first sight very beautiful. Approaching the island from the northward, it appears as a mass of rich green vegetation, the border of sea grape trees,[19] like so many bearded men,—whence its name was taken,—becoming more distinct as we approach. Towards its interior a succession of hills rise to a height of eight hundred or a thousand feet, their

---

18. On June 22, 1848.
19. *Coccoloba uvifera.*

95

sides mostly covered with turf, with here and there clumps of trees, the, intervening valleys divided by different estates and lots upon which are grown sugar-cane and guinea-corn.[20] The houses have such a home-like look that the name of "Little Scotland," long since given to the island, seems appropriate, more especially when the landscape is viewed from the summit of one of those hills inland, to which in one of our excursions we proceeded.

Unhappily a check—temporarily, it is hoped—has been brought upon the once flourishing sugar industry of the island. Since the emancipation of slaves took place, properties have altogether fallen in value, proprietors have been ruined, the universal complaint being that the freed slaves cannot be got to work. Geologically the chief component rocks of Barbados consist of coral limestone and coral. In respect to its fauna, it has the peculiarity of possessing but a small proportion of venomous snakes as compared with the other islands of the West India group. The people who have been born on the island are known as "Bims." Their colour is a mixture of red and albinoid white; their special characteristic said to be pride.

Comparing the climate of Barbados with that of tropical India, the former has various advantages. To a certain extent it is bracing and exhilarating; the prevailing breeze, as it comes across the Savannah, pleasant to the sensations, so that officers and other persons ride out at all hours of the day, their faces ruddy, themselves to all appearance in robust health. At intervals of seven to eight years, epidemics of yellow fever occur, such as that which recently attacked the 66th and 72nd Regiments, and after a temporary decrease in its severity, recurred with more than usual intensity and mortality.

With regard to physical conditions, geological and otherwise, there is to all appearance nothing of a kind to supply explanation, whether of the advent, increase, temporary cessation, sudden return with increased intensity, and final cessation; neither can explanation be drawn from those conditions for the lengthened duration of non-epidemic intervals, or of the cyclical re-

---

20. *Sorghum vulgare.*

turn of the disease in pestilential form.

Embarked on board the *Prince Royal* transport, I sailed for England. During the homeward voyage only one incident deserving notice occurred. In a clear moonlit night we became aware that we were in collision with a vessel of no great size. As we rushed on deck, we were shocked to observe that the craft suddenly disappeared a short distance astern of us. No less to his own surprise than ours, a sailor belonging to her was found on our deck, cast upon us in a portion of her rigging that lay across it. He was carefully seen to by us, taken to Portsmouth, and there handed over to the Spanish Consul, for we had ascertained that the ship run down had sailed from Corunna.

Gravesend reached, we disembarked; in due time reported our arrival at Headquarters. The authorities granted the usual period of leave of absence in accordance with Regulations at the time in force. From them also I received a letter conveying the thanks of Earl Grey for services performed in Africa. A few days thereafter I learned that of our "reliefs," three in number, two had died within a month after landing at Cape Coast, one of them my own successor. Fortunate, therefore, was my resolve not to delay departure.

Often is the statement made, but nearly always by persons who live at home at ease, that deaths of British officers in Africa and other tropical countries are due to their irregularities and vices, not to combined conditions collectively constituting climate.

The officers with whom I was associated on the Gold Coast were in their habits and general manner of life as nearly as possible like their contemporaries in England; nor did the few who at times exceeded somewhat appear to suffer in any respect more than did those of more temperate habits. It is the climate of Guinea, and it alone, that kills the white man, and in yet greater proportion the white woman.

An incident which occurred shortly after I had arrived in London was in its way illustrative of the state of public feeling at the time. It was while spending an evening in Portman

Street Barracks,[21] then occupied by the Scots Fusilier Guards, that orders from the Horse Guards directed that the battalion should be kept within barracks and under arms; information at the same time circulated that on the previous day there had been a "rising" of the Chartists at Ashton, near Birmingham, and that a similar outbreak in London was intended.

Subsequently we learned that the Duke of Wellington, then commander-in-chief, had made ample arrangements for such a contingency, though with so much secrecy and discretion that not a soldier was to be seen on the street. But the anticipated outbreak did not take place.

A portion of leave granted was devoted by me to the combined objects of restoring health and gaining knowledge. At the beginning of the winter session I re-entered at Edinburgh University to benefit by the lectures of Sir George Ballingall. Meanwhile, a friend [22] was interesting himself in appropriate quarters in view to my being released from further service on "the Coast."

21. With my friend J. A. Bostock.
22. General Sir Henry King, K.C.B.

CHAPTER 8

1848-1851. Ireland

Gazetted [1] to the 57th, I joined that distinguished regiment at Enniskillen, receiving from members of the "Die-hards" much civility and courtesy as a newcomer among them. A few months passed, and newspapers contained details of victory over the Sikhs at Chilianwallah,[2] though at a British cost in killed and wounded of 89 officers and 2,268 soldiers. With a sense of relief, intelligence by the following mail was read that crushing defeat had been inflicted upon the enemy at Goojerat,[3] though with a loss to our forces of 29 officers and 778 men; the dispersion of the beaten army, the flight of their Affghan allies towards the Khyber Pass—for disaffection on the part of Dost Mahomed had not yet been completely appeased.

During winter the weekly route march, with its attendant little incidents, furnished about the only events of regimental life that need be alluded to. As an outcome of what was looked upon as a scheme of "economical" administration proposed for political reasons, a reduction in regimental strength was ordered, several soldiers weeded out of the ranks in accordance with orders received. Not long thereafter public attention was drawn to "The Defenceless State of Great Britain" by Sir Francis Head, to whose book, so named, credit was given for measures speedily taken to reverse the schemes of reductions in *personnel* and

---

1. December 22, 1848.
2. January 13, 1849.
3. February 21.

matériel alluded to.

With the return of summer the routine of regimental life became again pleasant as compared with the monotony incidental to the dreary months of winter. The leave season over, the process of preparing for inspection seemed the only object for which the regiment existed, men and officers lived; for no sooner was the dreaded ordeal past and over, than the process was resumed for that which was to come six months later on. As so many interludes, entertainments given and received, games, and "matches "of various kinds became so frequent as to be looked upon as somewhat monotonous.

Exceptional in these respects was the anniversary, on May 16, of the battle of Albuhera in 1811, on which occasion the 57th Regiment earned the soubriquet of "The Die-hards," [4] of which it is so justly proud, the *esprit de corps* maintained thereby as well as through anniversary celebration being among its most valuable heritages. Then came the birthday of Her Majesty; after it, the celebration of Waterloo, "the credit of the regiment" being fully maintained on these occasions.

Trips in various, directions by water and land proved to be most enjoyable. Boating on the beautiful Loch Erne became a favourite pastime, picnics on some of the many islands with which it is dotted acquiring an interest of their own. Of those islands one has [5] a semi-sacred character; upon it stand ruins of an ancient church,[6] and, as believed, a still more ancient round tower. By road to Beleek [7] and Ballyshannon was no less pleasant and interesting. Around the promontory on which the first-named stands, the river Erne rushes as a magnificent torrent; the second noted on account of its "salmon leap," and legendary story connected with the islet[8] at a little distance seaward from

---

4. Out of 570 officers and men who went into action at Albuhera, the commanding officer, twenty-two other officers, and more than 200 men were placed *hors de combat*. The "dead were found lying as they fought in ranks; every wound was in front."
5. Davenish.
6. Dedicated to St. Molash, who died A.D. 563.
7. The manufacture of Beleek ware was then a thing of the future.
8. See *Illustrated London News,* October 12, 1849.

the cataract. Extending our trip to Sligo, we visited the ecclesiastical ruins and buildings pertaining to that city. In proximity to one of them, several small heaps of human bones lay among the grass, exposed to wind and weather. Inquiry elicited that they were exhumed remains of dead prior to 1832, the great mortality by cholera in that year rendering it necessary thus to "make room" for interment of the numerous victims. But the necessity for leaving exposed the vestiges of mortality was not apparent to us at the time.

At Bundoran I made the acquaintance of Lieutenant Monro, late of the Blues, living in retirement, his prospects ruined as a result of the duel into which he was forced with his brother-in-law, Lieutenant-Colonel Fawcett, 55th Regiment, whom he killed on that occasion. Coming as that duel did not long after the "meeting" between Hawkey and Seton, in which the latter received a wound that resulted in his death, public opinion became aroused against the practice. Within two years thereafter the Articles of War were so modified as to declare it to be a military offence on the part of an officer to fight a duel or fail to take measures to prevent one from taking place. For a considerable time past there had been a growing feeling in the army and in civil life against a system by which it was possible for the bully and the aggressor to have an advantage as a "professed duellist" over the less experienced adversary whom he might see fit to "call out."

The celebration of the victory of the Boyne, July 1, 1690, and that of Auchrim on 12th of the same month, 1691, was enthusiastically observed. Processions of men, bedecked with the distinctive colour of their party, led by bands of music and bearing with them a profusion of flags, paraded the streets of Enniskillen. From many windows orange flags and other party emblems were displayed; from the church steeple festoons of orange-coloured ribbons waved in the breeze. In other respects much of what was "demonstrative" in character took place, but the general impression produced upon strangers and uninterested spectators was not unlike that experienced as we looked in India upon "religious" festivals.

The visit of Her Majesty to Ireland, and the prospect of a *Levée* to take place in Dublin, attracted to that capital every officer whose duties and position admitted of his being temporarily absent from his regiment. The question of expediency of the Royal visit had for some time previous been subject of conversation, nor was there an absence of curiosity and anxiety in regard to the reception the Queen might meet with on the occasion of her traversing the streets. Everywhere it was enthusiastic, so much so. that Her Majesty was much impressed. The following day the *Levée* was held; some two thousand presentations were made, and in the list of those who had that honour my name was included.

At this time the general state of things in our immediate neighbourhood was this:—

The intensity of famine by reason of the potato blight of 1847-8 had to some degree become lessened; favourable summer weather had brought about an abundant crop of grain, relief works were in progress, the expenses of administration out of proportion to the meagre sums which actually reached the workers. All the while political and religious antipathies manifested themselves in violent forms; murders perpetrated in the close vicinity of our county town.

Some of the alleged perpetrators of those crimes underwent their trial at the County Assizes. Two were convicted and condemned to death. On the day of their execution a guard provided by the 57th was drawn up at a little distance from the main entrance of the prison, where the apparatus for carrying out the extreme sentence of the law was kept in readiness. Behind the soldiers the large open space then existing was crowded with interested spectators, the proportion of women being estimated as four to one of men. The dread ordeal over, one of our men was brought to the regimental hospital in a condition of delirious terror, his delusion that one of the men executed was dangling over his head. All means used to soothe or relieve him failed; his horrible delirium continued with little or no interruption through some few days and nights, only ceasing with his own existence, for the same terrible impression haunted him to the very last.

The system of "surprise inspections," at the time in force, applied to regiments and departments; inspecting officers were wont to appear without warning, such ordeals being over and above those held in ordinary course of routine. That the higher authorities saw good reasons for their action in this respect is not to be doubted. Those reasons, however, did not transpire; but among our soldiers the irritation caused by unusual proceeding went far to overbalance whatever good might have accrued from it.

On the 14th of March, 1850, the most sacred event of a man's life occurred in mine—that event, my marriage [9] to Annie, daughter of John Mackintosh, Esq., of Torrich. Time was pressing, for rumours were in the air that the regiment was well up the roster for foreign service. Leave of absence had accordingly to be curtailed; but, on rejoining the 57th with my young bride, she was received with the same kindness that had been shown to myself. Not many days thereafter, she proceeded to Dublin, where, pending the arrival of the regiment, including myself, she was most hospitably received by the family of a brother officer. [10]

Our progress to the Irish capital included several days' march; for, although railway communication could have been made use of for part of the distance, the authorities had decided that it should not be so. In our march, we passed through or were billeted for a night at places in relation to which history records a good deal of what is interesting. For example, Clones has an ecclesiastical history dating back to the sixth century; Kells, otherwise *Kenlis,* boasts of ruins of a monastery, said to have owed its foundation to St. Columba; in near proximity to Trim stands the rectory of Larour, the former residence of Dean Swift, and near

9. The ceremony solemnteed by the Rev. J. A. Grant, of Nairn.
10. Major and Mrs. Shadforth.

it a fragment of what had been the house of Stella. The ruins of Dangan Castle in the near neighbourhood were interesting, in that in them was shown to us an apartment said to have been the actual birthplace of the Duke of Wellington—with what degree of truth it was not deemed necessary to inquire.[11]

The village of Maynooth, at the time of our march through it, was in appearance wretched and decayed, even as compared to others along our line of route. At its eastern end is the avenue that leads to Carton, seat of Ireland's only duke.[12] But the name of the village has become associated with its Roman Catholic College, which dates from 1795, and was endowed by Sir Robert Peel[13] with an income yearly of £30,000—a measure much discussed at the time of our visit, as indeed it has continued since to be.

Arrived in Dublin, the barracks assigned to the 57th were the Linen Hall—old, and long before then condemned as unfit for occupation; accommodation for all ranks insufficient. Thus my experience in searching for lodgings began. Some months elapsed; then the regiment was "broken up," small parties distributed among various barracks, to be, after another interval, collected in the Royal Barracks—large, spacious, and, at the time, looked upon as well adapted for their purpose.

Duty, relaxation, pleasure, as represented in Ireland's capital, succeeded each other among our officers. In accordance with rules then in force, much of my own time was taken up in connection with the more military functions of parades, drills, field days, and ceremonial "trooping the colours." Regimental entertainments, levees, and "receptions" at the Castle were so many interludes in our general routine.

In accordance also with the custom of the time, civility and attention in various ways by learned societies and institutions were extended to medical officers of the garrison, myself includ-

11. Another statement is that his birth took place in Upper Merrion Street, Dublin; his baptism in St. Peter's Church.1
2. That was in 1850.
13. Parliament, June, 1845.

ed. Access to lectures in the Colleges was placed at our disposal; so was admission to the Botanical and Zoological Gardens. Invitations to picnics and to boating excursions in the beautiful bay further helped to render pleasant our stay in Dublin.

The once famous Donnybrook Fair[14] had not then become a thing of the past, although its extinction was approaching. The assemblage of people on the occasion comprised the wild in aspect, dirty in person, squalid, imperfectly clothed, all more or less strongly smelling of whisky, some dancing to music of their pipes; but so far as we saw, without the mirth, laughter, and other signs of Irish life of which we had heard so much.

Through the advocacy of Sir De Lacy Evans, and almost by it alone, officers of the Medical and Commissariat Departments were admitted to the second and third grades of the Most Honourable Order of the Bath.[15] In battles connected with recent campaigns, surgeons of British regiments were exposed to fire of the enemy in a degree only second to that of combatants, the casualties in killed and wounded among them testifying to the risks ran by them in the performance of their duties on those occasions. Other circumstances of military life tell more against medical officers of regiments than those whose duties are merely "combatant."

The combat over, the latter, if unscathed, takes his rest, such as it may be under the circumstances, but the most arduous duties of the former then begin. On marches incidental to campaigns, the halting ground reached, requirements of the sick and wounded must be attended to, often under great difficulties. In times of epidemics, the combatant runs risks common to all; the surgeon, in addition to them, is exposed to those incidental to close association with subjects of those epidemics, together with mental and physical wear and tear in the performance of professional duties. Hence arises the proportionately high rates of mortality that prevail among junior departmental ranks.

Some time thereafter, war was undertaken against the Kaffirs

14. August 31, 1850.
15. *London Gazette,* August 12, 1850.

under Sandilli, their chief. Eight infantry regiments were hastily dispatched to take part in the coming campaign, and so the 57th was placed among the first to proceed to the same destination in the event of reinforcements becoming necessary. Married officers, therefore, lost no time in forecasting arrangements to be made by them respectively in the event of the anticipated contingency becoming a reality.

My personal arrangements in that respect became hastened by the birth to me of a son.[16] Anticipating such an event, I had already opened negotiations for exchange to a regiment serving in India, conscious that colonial rates of pay and allowances were inadequate to meet the needs of double establishments during war time. By-and-by the time arrived when connection had to be severed with a regiment to which I had become much attached, and of its traditions proud as any other of its members. A farewell dinner, by invitation of Colonel Goldie [17] and officers, and then *adieu*.

---

16. Born on April 12, 1851.
17. Killed at Inkerman.

CHAPTER 9

1851-1852. Dublin to Wuzzeerabad

Among regiments stationed throughout the Punjab, then but
recently annexed, was the 10th Foot, to which, by exchange,[1] I
was now appointed. Towards that province I accordingly started
without delay. Arrived in London, we visited the great novelty of
that day, the palace of glass situated in Hyde Park, in which was
held the International Exhibition, progenitor of a long series as
it was destined to be. No time was lost in completing arrangements for the coming sea voyage in so far as restricted pecuniary
means permitted. Early in June we embarked on board the *Lord
George Bentinck,* I in charge of troops; some hours thereafter the
ship was under sail and away.

Among the incidents of our voyage these were recorded at the
time of their occurrence; namely, some of our crew drunk and
insubordinate, others impertinent; recruits undisciplined; junior
officers unacquainted with duties required of them. In a quarrel
between soldier and sailor the knife was used, fortunately without fatal result. The death-roll included one child, a soldier who
in *delirium tremens* jumped overboard, another who accidentally
fell into the sea during a squall at night,—his death-scream, as
he fell, most painful to hear.

Far away in southern latitudes (41^0 S.) we experienced a hurricane such as occur from time to time in those regions. Ten
days and nights it continued to rage; hatchways battened down;
men, women, and children confined 'tween decks, deprived to a

1. *London Gazette,* May 23, 1851.

great degree of light and air, their food and drink handed to and passed from each to other as best could be under the circumstances; decks washed from stem to stern by heavy seas, the ship running before the wind; sky so thick that "sights "were impracticable, and so our exact position left conjectural for the time being. This, added to experiences already mentioned, was the kind of initiation into the rougher side of military life to which my wife was subjected; she herself in delicate health, our infant son severely ill, his "nurse" a young untrained woman, the wife of a recruit.

The sea voyage ended, our detachment was conveyed by steamboat and flats to Chinsurah, as on a former occasion when transit was by means of country boats. Within a few days after arrival there, cholera attacked our young recruits, many of whom, as also the wives of some among them, fell victims. The sudden death of our child's nurse was the first shock and trying experience his mother had to face in India.

Starting on November 1, again by steamer and flats, our route was by the Sunderbunds to reach the main stream of the Ganges. A week previous that region was swept over by storm wave and hurricane, by which several ships, among them the steamer *Powerful,* were wrecked. Two days were occupied in passing along the narrow creeks that intersect the partially submerged forest tract, a thousand miles in superficial extent, to which the name of Sunderbunds is given. At the end of that time we are in the Ganges.

Time passed without special incident. Arrived at Purbootpore, a village on the left bank of the river,[2] the place was interesting only as being the locality where, on August 11, 1851, the Moolraj of Mooltan died, and was burned in accordance with Hindoo rites. He it was who instigated, in April, 1848, the murder of Vans Agnew and Anderson, and headed the revolt which led to the siege and capture of that fortress by British forces, and proved to be the first act in the second Sikh war of that year. The Moolraj was for upwards of two years detained as a political

2. On the twenty-second day of our river journey.

prisoner at Calcutta; his health having given way, Government sanctioned his transfer to Allahabad, and while on his way thither death overtook him.

Not far from Buxar we passed the point of junction between the river Kurumnassa and the Ganges. The former stream is by good Hindoos held accursed, so that to touch its water is to them pollution. This reputation, however, would seem to be of modern date,—namely, October 23, 1764, when the forces of Mir Cossim were defeated by those under Major Munro;[3] pursued by them to that river, in which many of them perished. It was a similar occurrence in 1826 on the part of the Ashantees at Acromanté that gave to that place in Guinea the name of "accursed," by which it was known during my period of service there.

In some respects our river voyage was pleasant; the cool dry air, the incidents of each day including walks on shore, the peculiarities of village life along the banks, the "fleets" and single craft we met, became, in turn, sources of interest to us. As this the dry season advanced, the size of the once mighty stream diminished, shoals became numerous, boats ran aground, delay and other inconvenience the consequences. On one such occasion several recruits from the particular boat concerned, started away clandestinely in the shallow water to indulge in the luxury of a river bath. Suddenly a scream was heard; two of their number disappeared; whether engulphed in a quicksand, or carried away by a crocodile, no one could tell.

Our river journey ended at Allahabad. Thence our progress was to be by march along the Grand Trunk Road. A short halt was permitted to enable officers to purchase such camp equipment and stores as pecuniary means were equal to.

Early in December we marched out of the—to me—familiar place. Nine days thereafter, arrived at Cawnpore, the terrible story in connection with which was in the not distant future. Here my wife had her first experience of one of those violent whirlwind storms whose distinctive name is taken from the lo-

---

3. Afterwards Sir Hector.

cality;[4] her surprise great on seeing some tents, articles of clothing, etc., drawn up and disappearing in the meteor.

At Kullianpore I found my way into the enclosure of a Hindoo temple. Great was my surprise at the offer of hospitality by the priests connected with it, they being in the act of partaking of a meal as I entered, the particular dish called "*phillouree.*" Of it accordingly I partook; but the incident seemed to indicate that then at least my hosts entertained no religious horror against the European.

Arrived at Meerut, the *Overland Express* brought news that "Louis Napoleon having the army on his side has carried all before him, dissolved the ministry and courts of law; has thrown himself on the people, and intimated his readiness to be designated by any title they may decide upon giving him." The next act in the drama so announced was soon to come.

Deobund was soon reached. There took place, in 1827, the last suttee permitted under public sanction. Since that date the practice has been officially suppressed, though it has been stated that isolated instances have clandestinely occurred. On the former *suttee* ground stood in its centre a temple; a series of small minarets of peculiar device indicate spots on which immolation of widows had taken place. The priests readily admitted us to the threshold of the shrine, but, unlike their brethren already mentioned, offered no food. In the neighbouring grove, numerous baboons—representatives of Humayon, the monkey god—chattered and made grimaces at us.

At Saharunpore a visit was paid to the Botanic Gardens. The excellence of their arrangement and management seemed to merit the eulogies bestowed upon them, a centre as they are from which plants are distributed throughout India, and to various European countries. The process of acclimatization was particularly interesting; so also was the care with which plants of temperate climates were being arranged and packed for dispatch to hill sanatoria in the Himalayas, there to remain throughout the coming hot season. It was a somewhat strange thing to see a

4. "Cawnpore devils."

daisy being thus nursed.

At Jugadree the detachment, its stores and equipment, crossed the Jumna, there so divided by shoals and islands as in effect to be four different rivers. Across the first the men waded at an hour so early that dawn had not appeared; the second and third were passed by means of bridges of boats such as are common on Indian rivers; over the fourth a bridge had been erected, so elegant in construction as to claim general admiration. Through its arches rushed currents of sparkling water, in the eddies and shallower parts of which were seen fish rising to flies; along the banks grew willow, acacia, and wild fig trees, the adjoining fields rich with well-irrigated crops of wheat. In the far distance rose above the haze of morning the snowy peaks of Himalayan.

Arrived at Umballah, headquarters of the Sirhind Division, a short halt was made, according to the custom of the time, for the double purpose of repairing equipage and exchanging draught animals where necessary. According also to the custom of the time, some of our number were invited to partake of friendly hospitality by officers stationed there.

Continuing, northward from Umballah were seen ruined remains of pillars raised by order of Jehangir[5] to mark the halting places of Noor Jehan, otherwise Noor Mahal, on her journey from Delhi to Lahore. Those remains seemed to occur at intervals of six to eight miles, representing the length of each daily journey of that *Chère Heine.*

Loodianah had an interest in that, during a severe cyclone some years previous, portions of barracks occupied by the 50th Regiment were blown down, several men being killed in the catastrophe, besides many injured. In the first Punjab war the Sikhs made a rush upon the station, set fire to and destroyed various bungalows and other buildings within it. Further depredations by them were checked by their defeat at Aliwal [6] by Sir Harry Smith.

Arrived at Kool, the position occupied by the army of Tej Singh preparatory to the battle at Ferozeshah, we mounted el-

---

5. Jehangir, A.D. 1605-1627.
6. January 28, 1846.

ephants and so rode to the field of that disastrous victory of December 21 and 22, 1845. Our ride for five miles was across open flat country, covered here and there by acacia bushes, occasional patches of cultivation occurring as we proceeded, the crops consisting of wheat and grain (*dolichos*).

The village of Ferozeshah, half concealed by groves, had yet some remains of entrenchments and batteries, behind and on which the Sikh guns were placed. Along the ground for a considerable distance in front of that position lay scattered and bleached by six years' exposure bones of gallant men, chiefly of the 62nd Regiment, for here it was that so many of them were swept away on the first of those eventful days. Of our small party there was one who had shared the risks and "glory" of that battle, and now pointed out the several positions occupied by the opposing forces.

Ferozepore, for many years the frontier station, ceased to be so when, after the battle of Sobraon,[7] British occupation of the Punjab took place. At one time a sandy plain, it had become beautified by ornamental trees and shrubs, and in other respects somewhat attractive in appearance.

Crossing in its near proximity the Sutlej—Hesudrus of the time of Alexander—we were within the territory of the Punjab—Panch-ab, or "Five Rivers." Five more marches and we encamped close to Lahore, capital city of that province; our camp pitched on ground where in former times had stood cantonments of troops in pay of Runjeet Singh. In near vicinity stood houses of British officials, some tombs and mosques, one of the latter transformed into an English church.

Arrived on the right bank of the Ravee (Hydraotis), our camp occupied ground close to the tomb of Jehangir, and not far from that of his empress Noor Jehan, "Light of the World," whose romantic history interested some of our number, if not all. Thence to Goojeranwallah, birthplace of Runjeet, "Lion of the Punjab," and anciently the Buddhistic capital of the province. In recent times the camp ground has obtained unpleasant

7. February 10, 1846. Punjab annexed, by Proclamation, March 29, 1849.

notoriety, it being so infected with poisonous snakes that a new site for that purpose has been selected.

Ten months' travel by sea and land, I joined the regiment into which, hoping thereby to advance my own prospects and position, it had cost me so much in means and personal trouble to exchange. Having done so, the occasion seemed opportune to take stock, as it were, of that position. At the date in question regimental appointments in India had their market value, according to their several kinds, and the period still unrun of service in that country. That of my own position was reckoned at; £100 for each year so before us; thus my exchange cost six and a half times that amount, in addition to which the cost of passage, added to other unavoidable expenses, placed me on the debit side to the extent of £1,180, all of which, having had to be "raised" as best I could, was an incubus to be got rid of with the least practicable delay. (Although anticipating the order of this narrative, the fact may be stated in this place that, by the aid of my dear wife and her patient submission to curtailment of luxuries and even necessities, pecuniary obligations were cleared off within eighteen months. As we shall see, troubles of other kinds arrived against which it became most difficult to bear up.)

CHAPTER 10

1852–1853. Wuzzeerabad

Immediately after the decisive battle of Goojerat,[1] by which
the Sikh army was completely overthrown, a position for troops
was selected on an extensive plain stretching for many miles
along and from the left bank of the Chenab.[2] That portion of
the plain chosen as a site for what were to be cantonments was
at the time under indigo cultivation; on it tents were pitched
and "lines" drawn out in accordance with regulations bearing
on the subject. With the approach of hot weather the tents were
walled and covered in by mud, straw, and such other materials
as under the circumstances were obtainable; then the tents were
struck, partitions of mud "run up," and so houses or bungalows
formed. By similar means "barracks" for the soldiers and their
establishments were erected; the whole declared to be the station of Wuzzeerabad.

Six miles away stood the city of that name; in its centre the
palace occupied by General Avitabile, in the service of Runjeet
Singh, and under him Governor of Peshawur at the time of the
first war against Affghanistan. Extending from the main entrance
to the city, what in former days must have been an imposing
avenue of trees is represented by dilapidated willow trunks; at
intervals smaller towns and villages occur, all surrounded by
richly cultivated fields. Across the river, said to attain a breadth
of fourteen miles during the rainy season, is seen the town of

1. February 20, 1849.
2. Chenab-Acesines.

Goojerat; towards our left the position of Chilianwallah; in the far distance the Pir-Punjal and other peaks pertaining to the Cashmere range of the Himalayahs.

Our force, equipped as a "Flying Column," was so held prepared and ready, if need arose, for emergent service. Rumour had it that among the people the state of things incidental to recent annexation did not meet with universal acceptance; that the system of Thuggee had extended to their country from Bengal, where for some years previous it had been relentlessly hunted down by Colonels Sleeman and Graham. At the new station of Sealkote an English church was in course of being erected. In reference thereto the strange report circulated among the natives that their children were being kidnapped, to be there offered as sacrifices. Meanwhile two expeditions were in progress of formation: the one to Swat, under command of Sir Colin Campbell; the other to Burmah, under that of General Godwin.

The hot season was soon upon us. As it advanced we became painfully aware how unsuitable, under the circumstances, were the extemporised "houses" already mentioned. By the aid of *tatties* and *thermantadotes*,[3] it was possible to reduce temperature within doors to something like 112^0 F.; but such contrivances were themselves expensive, and in some instances beyond the means of individuals. The sense of oppression from the prevailing heat was greater during the night than in daytime; the stillness of the air, laden with impalpable dust, affected not alone people, but quadrupeds and birds, while over everything a yellow haze lay thick and heavy.

Then would come a thunder burst; forked lightning threatened, and in some instances struck our houses; a downpour of rain would follow, and for a few days thereafter all would be comparatively agreeable. Later on hurricanes of dust burst upon us, their violence sufficient to unroof some houses and barracks, to be followed by storms of rain, and ultimately by the season so called. Early in September the hot season was at an end; the moist atmosphere became even more oppressive than it had

---

3. Composed of roots of the scented grass *Andropogon muricatum.*

been while dry heat prevailed, so that all of us looked forward anxiously to the advent of cold weather properly so called.

All belonging to the regiment suffered considerably in health; deaths of soldiers were numerous, the physical powers of all much depressed, a large proportion thus unfit to take the field in case of emergency. It was felt, however, that hospital *régime* was likely rather to increase their disability than benefit their condition; hence they were permitted to remain in barracks, though exempt from duty—a circumstance here noted as indicating the insufficiency of mere statistics to represent conditions of physical fitness of troops.

Among the deaths was that of a young surgeon,[4] only a few months in India when attacked by climatic illness, to which he succumbed. For some time before life passed away, incapable of expression by voice, his look of terror told plainly his state of mind as he faced approaching death. The scene was most painful to witness.

On September 5, '52, a daughter was born to me. The event took place in early morning. Shortly after midday information reached my beloved wife, through tittle-tattle of servants, that a guest,[5] who occupied a tent in our compound, was dead by heat apoplexy. Several of our men were struck down by the same disease, so that absence from my own domestic sphere was unavoidable under the trying circumstances of the day.

Within a week from her date of birth, an attempt was made by her *ayah* to poison the infant, the reason for the intended crime neither then nor subsequently ascertained. The prostrate mother from her bed saw the native woman put "something" in the mouth of the babe, who was immediately thereafter seized with tetanic spasms; nor was it without much difficulty that her young life was saved.

The recent discovery of gold-fields in Australia led to a somewhat unpleasant state of unrest on the part of a few soldiers serving in India. Letters from friends and relatives in the colonies

4. Jacob..
5. The young man may be indicated by his initials, J. C. G.

instigated them to endeavour by means, whether foul or fair, to get sent thither, where fortunes could very quickly be made. The result was the outbreak, as if epidemic, of crimes of assault on officers and non-commissioned officers, the idea being to get tried before a General Court-Martial and sentenced to transportation; after which, once in Australia, it would be an easy matter to find one's way to the gold-fields. This "gold fever "resulted in a Resolution by the commander-in-chief to put a stop to the assaults in question; in one instance—and it sufficed for the purpose in view—the death penalty awarded was carried out.[6]

On a morning in June, while examining a soldier who was about to appear before a Garrison Court-Martial on the charge of striking a sergeant, I received from the prisoner a somewhat severe blow on the forehead. Astonished at the occurrence, some little time was needed to collect my thoughts and decide upon the line of official action most suitable under the circumstances. In the interval I learned that the Garrison Court-Martial had been intentionally ordered to assemble for the express purpose of defeating the object the man was known to have in view, and this being the case it was natural to assume that in assaulting me he had in view trial and sentence by the more important tribunal.

Aware as I was that a sentence of death might be the possible award, and desiring to avert such a penalty, in making the official report of the assault I suggested that an inquiry should take place as to his mental condition at the time. Three months elapsed, and then the man appeared before that ordeal; he was found "not guilty" on the plea of "insanity." In due course he was sent to Calcutta, to be taken there into the Lunatic Asylum. At the end of a year he was discharged "cured" from that establishment, and while *en route* to rejoin the 10th he died of cholera. So ended that episode.

About the time I was struck a similar assault was committed upon the surgeon [7] of the 3rd Light Dragoons, occupying bar-

---

6. In a soldier of the 14th Hussars at Meerut.
7. Dr. Henderson.

racks also at Wuzzeerabad. He took steps to have an inquiry made into the mental condition of his assailant. On that inquiry I sat as president, and this is the substance of the story told me by the man. From the time when he first enlisted he had been haunted by visions of a murder committed by himself and his "pal" on Wandsworth Common in 1845; he made every endeavour to get killed while charging the Sikhs in battle; he had committed offences so that he might be taken to the guard room, and thence made pretended attempts to escape in the hope of being cut down by the sentry; but failing in all these he had struck the officer, in order that for so doing he might be tried, condemned, and shot. These particulars were duly entered in the report submitted to the authorities; meanwhile, the regiment to which he belonged received its orders for home, and left the station, taking with it as prisoner this unhappy man. It was not till long thereafter that the sequel of his story was heard of.

The death of the "Iron Duke" of Wellington, news of which was received early in November, was made the text of remark and discussion, the official acts and demeanour of His Grace towards officers and the army generally being looked at from different and at times directly opposite points of view,—the impression which seemed most generally to prevail being that although no one denied him the credit of great services performed in the first fifteen years of the century, yet for many years thereafter he had been "past his work"—a commentary which bears interpretation in more ways than one. It cannot be said that many signs of mourning for his loss were apparent.

Early in 1853 English papers brought news among other matters that Louis Napoleon had been recognised as Emperor by the Powers of Europe, though not with good grace, that a suspicion existed of a possible attempt at invasion was under consideration, an order for the concentration of troops of the regular army and militia at particular points being the outcome of that suspicion. Another item in those papers reads strangely while these notes are being transcribed, and conditions alluded to have developed in significance; namely, "The influence of the lower orders is fast on the increase, and altogether we seem to be on the eve of a crisis, the ultimate issue of which it is impossible to predict." Shortly thereafter came news of the Emperor's marriage to a Spanish lady,[8] his personal popularity in the army not enhanced thereby. According to Indian journals, overtures had been made to the British Resident at Moorshedabad by *Sirdars* of Affghanistan with a view to approach Government on the subject of taking over that kingdom. The truth or otherwise of the report did not transpire; but that the rumour was current was itself a suggestive circumstance.

As the hot season advanced, snakes, poisonous and otherwise, became numerous in cantonments. A *sepoy* while asleep was bitten by one of those reptiles. He soon became unconscious; blood oozed from two small punctures on the instep where he had been bitten, from his mouth, nostrils, and from under his finger-nails.[9] He was treated by means of large doses of ammonia and turpentine, and ultimately recovered.

Prowling beasts of prey made night hideous. On one occasion much alarm was occasioned by one of them becoming "rabid," rushing violently at and biting animals and people. Considerable numbers of both were so injured by the pariah dog; some of those bitten were treated, some not, but no specific results followed the injuries. In the bazaars within cantonments prowling jackals and wolves were so many dangers to infants asleep on *charpoys* at night; some instances occurred in which they were carried away and devoured by the larger animals mentioned.

The conditions of a soldier's life in India at the time alluded to were calculated rather to weary than enliven him. The climate ill suited for out-of-door exercise; many of the men unable to read, and disinclined to learn; their two resources the bazaar and the canteen; their tastes and pursuits animal; mind a blank; the body a ready prey to disease. Absolutely no good result was to be gained from official reports on these points, and suggestions for improvements. I addressed letters to the journals in the hope

8. Eugenie de Montijo, Comtess de Téba.
9. Indicating bite by Bungarus (Krite).

119

of enlisting attention in favour of station reading rooms, lecture rooms, etc., but with the result that little notice was taken of my representations. In the 10th Regiment itself, through the action of two or three officers, some of the soldiers enrolled their names as members of a "Mutual Improvement Society." Meetings were held; tea and other light refreshments served in view to attracting men; lectures and demonstrations given on such subjects as Forts and Battles mentioned in the Bible,[10] Strata of the Earth's Surface, Uses of the Human Body; classes for reading and writing also set on foot. Not long thereafter,, a general officer,[11] by order of the commander-in-chief,[12] arrived at Wuzzeerabad "to put a stop to so dangerous an association." Military opinion was not then ripened for the innovation.

After some delay, and with considerable difficulty, a Book Club for the soldiers was launched in the regiment; the officers were already well provided in that respect. As with the one class, so with the other, works on "service "subjects were mostly read, but intellectual occupation was thus available whereby to pass the weary and exhausting days of the hot season.

[Recollecting these endeavours made by a small number of us in 1853 to advance the intellectual condition of the British soldier in India, the few of us who still live attach suggestive significance to the extract now given from the most interesting work by Lord Roberts, entitled *Forty-one Years in India*.[13] Under the date 1887 he wrote:

My name appeared in the *Jubilee Gazette* as having been given the Grand Cross of the Indian Empire, but what I valued still more was the acceptance by the Government of India of my strong recommendation for the establishment of a Club or Institute in every British regiment and bat-

---

10. These lectures were given respectively by the Chaplain (Rev. Cave Browne), Engineer Officer (Captain Davidson), and myself.
11. The Honourable Thomas Ashburnham.
12. Sir Charles Napier.
13 Published in 1897. Vol. 2, p. 418.

tery in India. Lord Dufferin's Government met my views in the most liberal spirit, and, with the sanction of Lord Cross, 'The Regimental Institute' became a recognised establishment.]

The second hot season of our residence at Wuzzeerabad proved even more severe than the first upon the health of our soldiers, large numbers of whom suffered from illness special to the climate and locality. Unfortunately for those so prostrated, the apathy and indifference of the native servants connected with the hospital were such that many lives were thus sacrificed which under more favourable circumstances would in all probability have been saved. For example:—

A soldier in barracks, during the hottest hours of the day, is discovered by his comrades to be seized with heat apoplexy, or to be suffering from the scarcely less alarming symptoms of ardent fever. He is by them placed in a *dooly* and so dispatched to hospital. The bearers who carry him are indifferent to life and suffering among themselves, but if possible more so in respect to the white man, and so their pace is by no means rapid. They reach the "surgery"; but there, if they find no one present, they put their *dooly* down, while they themselves sit in the veranda to smoke, perhaps to sleep. After an interval more or less long, the presence of the sick—it may be unconscious—soldier is discovered; the circumstance, after another interval, comes, or is brought to the knowledge of the subordinate, who, just roused from his *siesta*, and considerably narcotised by his "*hookah*," takes time to collect his energies, and so be able to visit him. Even then the actual nature and severity of the attack is not always recognised and dealt with; so when the surgeon pays his evening visit, the patient is dead.

Among those struck down by severe illness was my dear wife, vitality brought to so low an ebb that only by holding a hand mirror to her lips and observing the slight moisture left thereon could the fact be realized that she still breathed. In this our time of trial, sympathy and aid came unexpectedly, but not from sources whence they were looked for as an outcome of services rendered. When her removal became practicable, she proceeded by *dooly dâk* towards Murree, then newly established as a hill station and sanatorium. Our cavalcade—for I was of the party—crossed the Chenab, partly by boat, partly by being carried through shallow water and marshy tracts. Arrived at Goojerat, the field of battle, at a little distance from the city, was found to be so overrun by vegetation as to be recognisable only by monuments to individual officers erected on spots where they had fallen. The day wore on; a messenger arrived, bringing, with "*salaam* from the Collector *Sahib*," [14] soup and other delicacies suitable for an invalid and infants. He had heard casually that a lady, severely ill, was in the *dâk* bungalow; hence this outcome of kind thoughtfulness towards complete strangers to him, as we were.

Jhelum, on the river so named, [15] was the next stage of our anxious journey. Thence, next night to Pucka Serai. Arrived at the *dâk* bungalow, it was found that the building intended for travellers consisted of one room; in it a single bedstead, on which lay an elderly field officer, who, in transit to the hills, had arrived shortly before us. Attendants were absent; supplies unobtainable; there was no alternative but to carry my sick wife from her *dooly* and place her alongside the sick officer. How the child and infant fared all day is not recorded.

Resuming our weary way as the cool breezes of evening set in, early morning found us at Rawul Pindee, then as still a favoured military station. Thence, in evening, towards the foot of the hilly range towards which our journey was directed. Night had closed in before the actual ascent began. As yet there existed no road properly so called. Progress was slow: rocks and boulders in the way caused many difficulties; but these surmounted, the light of our torches showed that in our progress we had attained a region of precipices, rugged valleys, and rapidly running streams.

As morning dawned we were set down at Trait, a place the

14. Mr. Sapte, long since passed away to the majority.
15. The Hydaspes of the ancients.

loveliness of which—surrounded by pine-covered hills; its rich green vegetation, the purling rivulets that traversed the valley, the coolness of the breeze that wafted over us—all these, delightful in themselves, exerted upon my wife an effect to be described as magical. Then it was that from her *dooly* the pale, emaciated form emerged. Enthusiastically she clutched a twig of pine tree I had just cut; its grateful resin scent brought to recollection associations of bygone days. From that moment her recovery began.

The further journey to Murree was continued, the cool air at the elevation of six to eight thousand feet, to which we had attained, enabling us to travel by day, instead of only by night as in the plains. A road was in course of being made, but as yet that by which we continued was little else than a rugged mountain path, leading upwards through forest composed of sycamore, pine, chestnut, and other trees familiar in our English woods; the altered conditions of temperature, scenery, and general surroundings were health-giving in their effect. Before many hours had passed we were welcomed and hospitably received by our friends, Dr. and Mrs. Banon.[16]

A few days elapsed, and through the station bazaar rumour circulated that on the 11th "a great earthquake would take place at Peshawur," "a native prophecy" having so declared. On the 13th information was received that on the 11th[17]—namely, the date indicated—Major Mackeson, Chief Political Officer at Peshawur, had been assassinated by an Affghan from Jallahabad; the murderer having delivered his thrust raised his hand to repeat the blow, when—so it was stated—a native rushed between them and received it. Subsequent information led to the belief that the murder of political officers at various other seats of local government had been intended, the existence of a conspiracy with that object well known among the native population.

Rejoining the 10th without delay, like every other officer who observed the signs of the times, I could not help seeing that as an immediate outcome of the Peshawur murder, the aspect

---

16. On September 1, 1853.
17. Telegraphic communication did not then exist.

of public affairs, not only on the North-Western frontier, but throughout India, rapidly became such as to cause anxiety to administrators, while it led officers and soldiers to speculate on the chances of active service. The prime mover in the murder of Major Mackeson was believed to be Sadhut Khan, chief of the Lalpoora State. Immediately on the occurrence of the murder British troops were moved onwards from Rawul Pindee, orders issued for others to march from other stations to take their place.

These proceedings occupied several days, as all such movements had to be performed on foot. In the meantime the troops arriving at Peshawur were received with signs of disaffection by the Mahomedans of that city; while Rawul Pindee, left for the time being with a diminished garrison, was threatened with attack by a band of Hazara men under an impostor named Peshora Singh,[18] who pretended to be a son of Runjeet Singh. That attack did not take place, but a movement somewhat threatening in character was made towards Murree, at the time occupied by invalid soldiers and their families, wives of officers (mine included), and the small number of officials required for the inconsiderable dimensions it had then attained.

On the night of September 28, some hours after darkness had closed in, messengers sent round for that purpose spread the alarm throughout that station that the Hazarees were rapidly advancing up the hill towards it; orders at the same time issued by which all should forthwith repair to the residence of the Commissioner, leaving their houses "standing." A heavy thunderstorm prevailed at the time; lightning flashes at intervals lit up the miry pathways along which the ladies and children had perforce to walk, in some instances a distance of a couple of miles.

My own dear wife, as yet unrecovered, and unequal to such an exertion, was carried, together with her two children, and so reached the general rendezvous, where earlier arrivals had barricaded themselves as best they could by means of tables, chairs,

19. Peshora Singh was drowned in the Indus.
20. Mr. Thornton.

and other articles of furniture. Meanwhile the Commissioner[19] collected such officers, soldiers, and police as could be brought together in the emergency. Marching as best they could in the darkness, they came in contact with the rebels at daylight, and after a smart skirmish dispersed them, the Commissioner being wounded in the *rencontre*.

By the middle of October my wife, though far from restored to health, was sufficiently well to return with her two children to the plains. Starting from Murree in the evening, her palanquin-bearers speedily showed themselves to be ill-disposed; while she, unprovided with a guard, as some other ladies had been, was rendered helpless in what proved to be a most painful position. Frequent halts, unnecessary delays, repeated demands for *buxees* (presents), and general disregard of her requests to keep the *palanquins* together, continued throughout the long dreary hours of darkness, and well on in the following day.

It was afternoon before she was deposited at the *dâk* bungalow of Rawul Pindee; but the party conveying her infant was nowhere in sight, nor could tidings of it be obtained. Thus did several hours pass. Then it was that the arrival of an officer[21] enabled my wife to communicate to him her state of anxiety and alarm. Without delay he proceeded to the residence of General Breton, in command, with the result that a cavalry escort was dispatched in search of the missing ones. Another period of delay, fear, and anxiety, and the palanquin with the infant arrived. It appeared that her carriers had simply deposited her on the road-side in the jungle, and dispersed. What might have happened is painful to contemplate.

For some time past a charitable hospital for the benefit of the native population in and around cantonments had been maintained by subscriptions and other contributions from officers of our regiments, the professional duties connected therewith being performed by myself. Gratitude on the part of those who benefitted by that institution was never expressed verbally, and in many instances not at all; indeed, claims were in some made

---

21. Captain, afterwards General Sir William Payne, K.C.B.

for pecuniary reward, on the plea that individuals had submitted themselves to be operated upon. In a few instances, however, active gratitude was expressed, even in a somewhat demonstrative manner. The use of chloroform was then in its very early stages. In the instance of a child, that anaesthetic was administered while it lay placidly in its mother's arms. When under the influence of the drug, the little patient was gently lifted, placed upon a table, operated upon,[22] then replaced in the position from which it had been taken, still apparently asleep, and placid. The surprise of the mother was very great; the whole thing declared by her to be *jadoo*—that is, witchcraft!

---

13. Lithotomy.

CHAPTER 11

1854-1856. Meean Meer

After a succession of orders and counter-orders, the 10th marched away[1] from Wuzzeerabad; on the eighth day thereafter entered the recently erected and spacious barracks of Meean Meer. On the extensive plain where they stand, the Khalsa army assembled in 1845, prior to the "invasion of India" by them, and prior to that date quarters there existed for the troops of Runjeet Singh. On the same plain in 1846, the victorious army under Lord Gough encamped, and so commanded Lahore, situated some six miles distant. The name of the locality is that of a saint, a native of Bukkur in Scinde, who flourished in the time of Jehangir,[2] and whose tomb still remains in tolerable repair.

Among those who died in the early part of 1854 was the Brigadier commanding,[3] an old officer whose service in India had extended over about fifty years. He represented a class, then somewhat numerous, of men who had proceeded to that country while as yet in their teens, and thenceforward spent the whole or greater part of their lives in it. The funeral was performed with full military honours; but what struck us as incongruous and out of place was the suddenness with which, after it had been completed, the strains of "The Dead March "were succeeded by those of what were described as "rollicking" airs. Surely, under such circumstances, it would be more appropriate

---

1. On November 15, 1853; arrived on 23rd.
2. A.D. 1605-1627.
3. Sir James Tennant, K.C.B.

127

were the troops marched back in silence to their barracks.

Unhappily a painful state of "tension "had for some time previous existed in relations between the officer in command and those immediately under him; confidence was seriously impaired among all grades; actions and "system" of the superior looked upon as capricious, influenced by personal feelings, and, in some instances, tyrannical. The outcome of all this was, in respect to those affected, a condition very difficult to be borne, an existence approaching the miserable in, place of one of friendly communication after the manner of regiments in general. Among the ranks there was reason to believe that attempts had been made, and others contemplated, against the objectional life. The following incident was suggestive under the circumstances of the time. A soldier came to hospital; a man of good character, long service, and known never to shirk duty. To the usual question, "What is the matter with you?" he answered, "Nothing, sir."

Then, "What brings you here?"

"Because I am harassed and worried to death, and have come to ask if you can give me a day or two's rest."

His request was acceded to, and so, in all probability, a serious crime averted.

In the middle of March a Lahore newspaper published what was the first telegraphic[4] intelligence ever received in this part of India. According to that intelligence, the Russian Ambassador to England had taken his departure from London; France and England were dispatching troops in view to joint action in support of Turkey, those from our own country comprising twenty-two battalions, and so leaving only eleven, exclusive of Household troops, in home garrisons. A month later came the further news that all the forces in the United Kingdom were under orders of readiness for service; that a powerful fleet had been mobilised; the army materially augmented, several regiments recalled from the West Indies, and the fleet dispatched to the Baltic.

On 30th of March a son [5] was born to me by my beloved

4. Called by the natives "*Bijlee ke dâk*," or "Lightning Mail."
5. Baptized on April 24, 1854.

wife, as I wrote at the time—another hostage to Fortune, and very material inducement for exertion on my part to earn, if possible, means whereby to maintain and educate my children in such a manner as is incumbent upon me. The state of her health required that with the least practicable delay she should proceed to the hills. A house was engaged at Simla for the season, and there she passed the greater part of the hot months.

My health having given way, I proceeded to that sanatorium somewhat later in the hot season. Forty miles from the plains, and 7,600 feet above sea level, the climate of Simla is agreeably cool, but rain so heavy that during the three months of summer the fall amounts to 100 inches. In the faces of declivities from rocks and mountain spurs grew deodars and rhododendrons, intermingled with wild apple, cherry, holly, walnut, etc.; orchids, ferns, ivy, and woodbine.

Small but rapid streams pursue their tortuous course over their rocky beds in each narrow valley, and at a distance of some two or three miles are two cascades of some 70 and 120 feet in height. Away in the distance the magnificence of the snowy range, consisting of what seems like an interminable succession of white glistening peaks, fixes the mind in wonder and admiration; while in a clear day it is possible to see the plains, together with the windings of the river Sutlej.

The "inauguration"—otherwise commencement—of what was to be the great canal uniting the Ganges and the Jumna was duly celebrated. The subject of that canal was discussed in the public papers from different points of view; the channel, while intended to irrigate many tracts that stand in need of being so fertilised, would be used in places where such aid to agriculture was not required, and in certain localities "malaria "would appear where none now exists. It may be curious to compare those predictions with the results of experience.

Somewhat later in the year a Cheap Postage Act came into operation in India, according to the system adopted in England since 1841. Another matter noted at the time had reference solely to the army; namely, that an entire change took place in the uniform of soldiers and officers, one item relating to which was that thenceforward the infantry were directed to leave the upper lip unshaven,—in other words, to grow *moustachios*.[6]

In the middle of October my wife and children arrived from the hills. With health restored she was able to enjoy rides and other excursions around our station, the crisp morning air of the Punjab restoring to her cheeks, as to those of others that had become pallid, the rosy tinge natural to them. The frequency with which field-days and other great military displays took place—for our force numbered 13,000 fighting men—gave her, with other ladies, opportunities of being present on such occasions, and entertainments of sorts furnished us with an object or excuse to visit what were then the well-kept and ornamental gardens of Shalimar, the original planning of which is credited to Sultan Beg, an "Admiral of the Fleet" to Shah Jehan:

Occasional visits had to be made to Lahore, the history of which city presenting many points of interest, a few particulars relating thereto may be interpolated in this place. Surrounded by a line of ramparts now dismantled and rapidly going to decay, sufficient remains to indicate the great strength of the original fortifications. At regular intervals there are gateways, at each of which a strong guard was formerly posted for defence. Through one such gate we entered, and were immediately in a labyrinth of narrow and crowded streets. The houses, built partly of brick, partly of sandstone, are three and four stories in height, their fronts more or less elaborately ornamented by carvings of different kinds, but all such devices presenting evidence of decay.

What formerly was the palace of Dyhan Singh is now a pay office for British troops. The Shish Mahal, or Glass Palace, is much defaced; the precious stones of its mosaic work taken away, the spaces at one time occupied by them giving to the whole an aspect of dilapidation even beyond what has actually taken place. What was the audience hall, however, remains in good repair, the walls and roof ornamented by mirrors of various sizes, some set in silver frames, others in those of gold, the whole

6. By orders dated Horse Guards, October 7, 1854.

interspersed with paintings done in the most gorgeous colours. But how changed the style of occupants now from that which in days gone by harmonized with such surroundings!

As we entered, there sat upon the marble floor a motley crowd of Sikhs, men and women, old and young, their costumes betokening that they were of the labouring classes; the mission that brought them hither to receive, at the hands of representatives of the great Company Bahadur, pensions for sons, husbands, or fathers who fell in battle against that wonderful and mysterious abstraction known to "the masses" of India only by that designation. In close vicinity to the Shish Mahal was a large mosque, very similar in style and appearance to the Jumna Musjid at Delhi; it was now occupied as a magazine.

Thence we proceeded to the gateway where a few years ago Rajah Nao Nehal Singh lost his life,—whether by accident or design is still by some few persons considered doubtful. Adjoining that gate stands the tomb of Runjeet Singh, on entering which we found two priests ready to give whatever aid the Feringhee might stand in need of. Under a coverlet of green cloth the Grunth, or Holy Book of the Sikhs, was carefully preserved; but the cloth was raised for us, so that we might look upon the sacred volume.

In a shrine under an unfinished dome within the temple or tomb, the ashes of Runjeet were preserved, the shrine itself concealed under a green cloth; the walls of the mausoleum covered with paintings and other representations of Sikh mythology. In another building, though of less artistic appearance than that mentioned, were preserved the ashes of Nao Nehal Singh and of Soochet Singh; between the two shrines containing them lay covered as before the Grunth.

In the last week of October came news that the Russian camp before Sebastopol had been forced, but with a loss to the allied forces of 2,500 in killed and wounded. Many of us, besides the interest natural to the important events then taking place in the Crimea, had personal acquaintances among the actors in the drama of war there in progress, and were moreover conscious of an existing possibility that we also might be transferred to that sphere of action—a possibility looked at from various points Of view, according to circumstances, pecuniary and matrimonial, of individual officers.

The Indian papers of the day gave currency to a report that our quondam ally and prisoner Dost Mahomed had been making endeavours, by means of *vakeels*, to sound the Indian Government in regard to an alliance, offensive and defensive; intimating at the same time the possibility of his coming to terms with Russia, should his proposal be rejected. But according to the views expressed at the time, little danger was apprehended in the North-West,—that is, from Russia,—on account of the natural mountain barrier that serves as a defence in that direction.

Early in 1855 news reached us that Inkerman had been won[7] by our troops, though at a cost to those engaged of 2,600 in killed and wounded out of 6,000, the 57th being among the heaviest sufferers. Several regiments[8] had already been sent direct from India to the Crimea; the 10th expecting to follow to the same destination, officers and soldiers composing it held themselves prepared for such an emergency, which however did not occur. Among ourselves the chances of service nearer at hand were freely discussed, as were possible risks that might attend the further withdrawal of troops from India. That a state of unrest existed was declared from day to day in the columns of the local papers, and was evident to all who chose to pay attention to palpable indications. Few, if any, of us at the time gave a thought to the conditions to which that unrest was due, nor to the outbreak in which it was so soon to culminate.

All ranks and grades pertaining to regiments were interested in the varying phases of public affairs, their personal comfort, convenience, and possible prospects being likely to be affected thereby. For some time past Persia had treated British representatives with growing marks of disrespect, and now the circum-

---

7. November 5, 1854.
8. Namely, 22nd, 96th, and 98th Regiments, 10th Hussars, and 12th Lancers.

stance led to the withdrawal from Teheran of the Commissioner of Her Majesty at that capital. There were, moreover, suspicions of an intended movement on Herat, in accordance, as believed, with Russian instigation; consequently, the early dispatch of an expedition was looked upon as a probable contingency,—the object, according to one set of views, to "assist" the Shah; according to another, to coerce him. Speculation was indulged in as to the regiments most likely to be so employed, "ours" being considered one of the most likely to be so. Our arrangements were made accordingly; but a year had to elapse before war was actually declared.

In the month of July (1855) came the unexpected news that the Santhals had broken out in rebellion. We asked each other, Who are the Santhals? They were a half-savage tribe inhabiting the Rajmahal Hills; nor was it possible at the time to ascertain the ostensible cause of their outbreak. The troops sent against them consisted of a local corps,[9] composed of their own tribesmen, the natural result being that they fraternised with the rebels. The next "force" dispatched to quell the outbreak was a body of *sepoys* of the 7th Native Infantry,[10] and they, it was reported, fired over the heads of the rebels, their officers using their fists upon the men who did so.[11] Meanwhile the rebellion spread; depredations and murders were committed wholesale. Martial law was proclaimed in the disturbed districts; troops were employed during seven months against men armed to a great extent with bows and arrows; at last the guerrilla warfare was brought to a close. The inaction of the *sepoys* on the occasion alluded to became significant some time thereafter when the great mutiny occurred.

The death of the Czar and accession to the Russian throne of Alexander were the most important items of intelligence brought by the mail arriving early in April; another, his expressed determination to continue the war with vigour. Other items of

---

9. Bhaugulpore Hill Rangers.
10. Together with 8th and 40th Native Infantry, mutinied at Dinapore in 1857. 11. *Delhi Gazette.*

intelligence noted at the time as having more or less important bearings upon affairs in India, included the withdrawal of Lord Aberdeen from the Ministry and the appointment of Lord Palmerston as his successor; the death of Joseph Hume, who, it was remembered, had begun his career in the Burmese war of 1824-26; and lastly, the cross-fire between Admiral Sir Charles Napier, on his return from Cronstadt, and Sir James Graham, the First Lord of the Admiralty. Then came details of the attacks on the Mamelon and Malakoff Towers, and of the losses incurred by our troops, more especially by the 57th. Following thereon, intelligence arrived of the outbreak of cholera among the allies in the Crimea, and of the death thereby of Lord Raglan.

In the early days of September, the serious illness of my wife at Simla rendered it necessary that I should proceed thither without delay. On the journey all went well, till on arriving at the river Beas—the Hyphasis of the ancients—the *palkee* in which I was being conveyed across, by means of a boat, was by some mischance permitted to fall into the stream, after which accident, time so pressed that without interruption I continued my journey.

Arrived at the foot of the hills, I mounted a horse, and, lantern in hand,—for night had now closed in,—I proceeded along the rough footpath which then was the only representative of a road. Soon the darkness was absolute; the roughness of the pathway had increased; the thick jungle was close to me on either side. Then it was that my steed stumbled and fell; myself and lantern were on the ground; my light extinguished. In this condition of things I perforce remained a considerable time, until a party of pedestrians, having at their head a torch-bearer, came upon me. I was glad to return with them to the nearest staging bungalow, and there remain till morning. Next day I resumed my journey. I reached my destination tired and feeling much indisposed.

Five days thereafter I was seized with what proved to be a most serious illness. One day of intense headache, another of shivering, then prostration, then delirium, after which a blank of more than a couple of weeks. Such were the results of this untoward journey. During those days and nights of delirium, a succession of very horrible dreams, hallucinations or mental wanderings haunted me, one of the most painful being that everything in my room—bed, tables, chairs, etc.—was alive, and that I myself was double; at the same time I was haunted with an intensely strong desire to die. In the third week of my illness my state was so far improved that I was able to sit up in bed, but only for a few minutes in the day. During this trying and anxious time to my dear wife, she had to tend me, not only by day, but also at night; her servant, the wife of a soldier, assisting her. It was in these circumstances that she gave birth to a son on October 7.

Weak in body, and ill as I was, my wife far from recovered, with the additional charge of a baby to that of a sick husband, we left Simla on October 26; in due time arrived at Umballah, and on November 4 joined my regiment there, it being *en route* to Dinapore. The following day I underwent the ordeal of having the uvula cut off, that organ having become so elongated during the severity of my illness as by constantly irritating the throat to add to the severe cough and lung complication which formed part of my illness. Much of our march was by road already traversed.

Our usual hour of starting ranged from three to four in the morning; we had to rise at least an hour before that time, and I well remember how on such occasions my dear wife, herself very ill-fitted by reason of the weak state of her health, prepared for me a cup of egg-flip, and so enabled me to bear removal from my camp bed to the *dooly* in which I travelled. But as we marched from day to day, health so far recovered that I became able to walk some little distance at a time by means of a stick. My left lower limb was much the weaker of the two, but at first I failed to perceive that it was to some degree paralysed.

On Christmas Day our young infant was observed to be somewhat ill. With great rapidity his symptoms increased in severity, and on the last day of the year death came as a relief to his sufferings. As soon as practicable after the severity of his illness declared itself, we hurried on from camp to the *dâk* bungalow at Barode, and there the dear innocent babe passed away to his rest. The thought of leaving the remains of our loved one in the jungle was horrible; we accordingly procured such a coffin as could be roughly put together by the bazaar carpenter, and with our melancholy burthen pushed on to Benares, where we arrived at 1 a.m. on New Year's Day. It was not, however, until sunset of the same day that arrangements for the interment were completed, and the remains reverently committed to earth in the Military Cemetery.

Four months elapsed, illness still prostrated me. Recovery was little likely to occur while I remained in India; consequently there was no alternative but to proceed on sick leave to England. On arriving at Calcutta, much difficulty was experienced on obtaining temporary accommodation, the hotels and other establishments being full. After some delay quarters in Fort William were assigned to me; furniture and equipment obtained on hire, and so I waited until official routine had been gone through, and authority granted for my departure.

For some time past the contemplated annexation of Oude was known throughout the military stations of India. The carrying out of that intention was naturally looked forward to as likely to result in a force being assembled, and perhaps engaged on active service. My own incapacity to take part in any such service was a severe disappointment. When, added to my physical condition, the fact that pecuniary affairs had not yet emerged from a state of difficulty, and that prospects were far from bright as to health being ever restored sufficiently to enable me to meet responsibilities attached to me as "bread-winner," the general survey of the position in which I stood was decidedly depressing. In one respect it was a relief to me to learn that all chances of service had been averted; that Oude had been annexed without the necessity for sacrificing life—at that time at least.

In the suite of rooms adjoining ours in Fort William an officer was suddenly seized with cholera, the attack rapidly progressing to his death. After that event his young wife, who had been constant in her attentions to him, observed his fingers move spasmodically, as often happens in such cases; thereupon she rushed to the medical officer in attendance, exclaiming frantically, "He lives, he lives; why say you that he is dead?" Nor was it easy to convince her that her hopes were vain,—that he had gone to his rest. The scene was altogether a very painful one to witness, though one by no means uncommon in India.

Suffering as I was from physical weakness, and conscious of the possibilities that might happen to those dependent upon me, in the probable contingency which now presented itself vividly to my mind, the fact that for some days I became prostrated under the influences then prevailing was no surprise to myself. On the 5th of March the *Marlborough,* in which we had embarked the previous afternoon, started in tow of a steamer; but what between breakdowns and other mishaps, it was not until the 17th—St. Patrick's Day—that our homeward voyage really began.

The voyage was by no means propitious, for, as noted at the time various causes of discomfort and inconvenience were at work. Scarcely had we got to sea before the woman engaged to attend our children became ill, and so gave up her work; mumps and whooping-cough affected nearly every child on board; my eldest had a tedious attack of fever; my wife became ill, partly from arduous attendance on the children, partly from the unwholesome conditions on board.

Gradually there had become perceptible a stench, which in its intensity affected seriously the health of the people on board, and rendered discoloured the white-lead paint throughout the vessel, the plated dishes, and articles in personal wear. Pumps were set to work and kept continually in use; myriads of maggots were thus taken up with the bilge-water, proving the existence in the depths of the vessel of animal matter in a state of decomposition.

A formal representation by the officer[12] commanding the invalids on board and myself to the captain was made on the

12. Colonel Blachford, 24th Regiment.

subject, with a request that he would put in at Delagoa Bay. That representation was ignored; and so the remaining portion of the voyage had to be got over, the conditions just mentioned having, as expressed, "to wear themselves out."

On the 1st of July we passed the Azores at so short a distance from them that we were able to enjoy the view of those beautiful islands. Nearing Plymouth, our ship was boarded by a venerable pilot, who, though seventy years of age, was actively employed in his responsible and arduous vocation. On the 14th of that month we reached Gravesend, and there disembarked; my wife infirm in health, two of our children unrecovered from their attacks of illness while on board, myself with one limb disabled, my physical condition to a great extent wrecked.

In due course the ordeal of a Medical Board was gone through; the members of that body were able to appraise the significance of that condition, but in accordance with "the system" of the day were unable to recommend leave of absence for any longer period than three months—a period obviously insufficient for restoration to health and activity.

A few weeks were spent in travelling in search of health. The fact being evident that further leave must be applied for in due time, the climate of Aberdeen was selected as one suited to my then condition; in that city, accordingly, we remained for several successive months, with result as anticipated, that the bracing winter air proved to be health-restoring and invigorating, though the period during which I was permitted to enjoy it was insufficient for its full benefit being obtained. In various ways civility was shown to us by residents. On the winter "session" at Marischal College being opened, a kind invitation was sent to me by Dr. Pirie to attend his lectures. Little thought I at the time how soon some of the valuable teaching communicated in those lectures was to be practically applied.

CHAPTER 12

1857. Aberdeen—Dinapore
—Outbreak of Sepoy Mutiny

The year 1857 began with me inauspiciously. Unrecovered from illness, it was necessary that I should proceed to the metropolis, there to appear before a Medical Board. A short extension of leave being granted by that tribunal, the fact was communicated in a manner personally offensive, with the intimation superadded that if at the expiration of the period I was still unfit to join my regiment, I must make way for a more efficient officer.

The aspect of affairs, so far as I was concerned, was gloomy. On the one hand I had the prospect of half-pay for an indefinite time, on a rate[1] quite insufficient to meet the ordinary needs of myself and family; on the other, to return to India in the state of physical illness in which I then was. Taking an estimate of my worldly means, the circumstance came out that from insurance, and small amount of investments as they then stood, comparing the result with income on half-pay, the receipts of my wife as a widow would exceed by a trifling amount that to which I should be entitled in the alternative first named. Thereupon decision was quickly made; a solicitor prepared my "last will and testament." I placed the document in the writing portfolio of my wife; took leave of her as she lay weak and ill in bed;[2] started

1. Of 8s. per day.
2. A son born on March 14, 1857.

away to rejoin my regiment, the children clapping their little hands as I did so, and shouting, "Papa's gone away for toys."

Embarking[3] at Gravesend, the earlier part of our voyage was without special incident. The excellent selection of books sent on board for the use of the troops—for a considerable number were being conveyed to India—enabled those who so desired to get through a good deal of reading. A passage in one of those works seemed so appropriate at the time to personal conditions that it was duly noted; namely,

> The evil we suffer is often a counter-check which restrains us from greater evil, or a spur to stimulate us to good. We should therefore consider everything, not according to present sensation of pain, or the present loss or injury it occasions, but according to its more general, remote, and permanent effects and bearings—whether our higher faculties are not brought more into play, and our mental powers more invigorated by the meditation and experiments necessary to secure ourselves. [4]

A considerable part of the voyage passed without special incident. Some "heavy" weather was experienced, but in that respect nothing unusual or of a kind likely to do harm to ship or stores. Great, therefore, was the consternation with which we learnt that water casks and tanks had so suffered that the sea water had got into and rendered their contents unusable. At the time we were in the latitude of the Mauritius, and about twelve hundred miles east of that island.

What was to be done? The chief officer and myself devised a distilling apparatus, constructed with kettles, boilers, gun-barrels, and leaden pipes of sorts. Our success was considerable; some twenty gallons of "fresh" water were thus obtained throughout the day, and so on during twenty-two that had to pass before land was reached, though from some of our lady passengers comments were not wanting as to the "nasty" taste of the product.

3. The *Palmyra*.
4. *Entomology*, Kirby and Spence.

Meanwhile fuel ran short; bulkheads and spars had to be utilised; our ship reduced to skeleton state. In that condition we arrived off Madras and anchored.

The news we there received was at the moment astounding, as it was unexpected. The greater part of the Bengal army in open mutiny; *sepoys* murdering their officers, together with their wives and children; widespread disaffection among the native troops of both the other Presidencies. As written at the time, and when the intelligence was fresh:

"It appears that the ostensible cause of the outbreak was the issue of cartridges greased with animal fat. But for a long time past a deep-rooted determination has existed among the natives to throw off a foreign yoke, and to raise for themselves a king of the Delhi line of succession. Large numbers of mutineers are said to have fled to the imperial city; many officers and their families have been massacred."

At Madras the state of things indicated that something very serious and unusual was in progress. European residents enrolled as volunteers; Fort St. George in process of being manned and provisioned; ammunition got ready for immediate use; at each post where stood a native sentry there was also placed a British soldier, or pensioner, the latter "embodied" and armed for the occasion. The regiment[5] in the fort was held ready for emergencies; so were the artillery at St. Thomas' Mount. The Mahomedan inhabitants of Triplicane, a suburb of Madras, were declared to be in open revolt.

At the mouth of the Hooghly the arrival of the pilot on board was eagerly looked for, his recital of news listened to with painful interest. In that recital particulars were given of murder and atrocities[6] committed by mutineers on women and children, the names of the victims at the same time given. Disembarking at Calcutta early in August, unusual military turmoil was in progress. At short intervals throughout the city parties of extemporised volunteers were posted; Fort William was in course of

5. The 43rd Light Infantry.
6. Hosea 13. 16.

reinforcement; the streets were patrolled by armed parties of Europeans, while everywhere an air of unrest seemed to prevail. At Government House sentries of the Body Guard were on duty, their arms the ramrods of their carbines. An impression existed that as the date was that of the Mahomedan festival, the Buckra-eed,[7] the occasion was likely to be celebrated by an attack on the capital—a belief which derived support from the fact that a spy from the King of Oude, then at Garden Reach, had been captured while conveying a traitorous letter, his trial and execution following thereupon without much delay.

Other preparations in progress indicated the conditions of the time; accommodation, stores of food and clothing, as well as other requirements, were being got ready in anticipation of women and children, survivors from deeds of blood at upcountry stations, who were known to be on their way hither. Comments were very freely made on the energy displayed by commanders in some instances, in contrast with pusillanimity in others.

A passage order obtained, I embarked as deck passenger—for there was no spare cabin—on board the river fiat *Soorma,* proceeding with a body of Sikh troops and their officers, Sir James Outram and staff being in the steamer to which the *Soorma* was connected. On the day of our departure we met in the Hooghly a steamer and its flat, both crowded with ladies and children who had succeeded in effecting their escape, but whose husbands, fathers, or other relations had for the most part fallen victims at their respective stations. Very terrible were the tales some of the "refugees," as they were called, told of atrocities committed within their own knowledge, or of which they had received what in their estimate was authentic information. A few examples must suffice:—

Two young ladies[8] stripped naked, tied to *hackeries,* and so driven through the streets, then dishonoured by sweep-

---

7. Buckra-eed. In commemoration of the sacrifice by Abraham, according to the Koran, of Ishmael, child of his bondswoman.
8. Names of these and other victims to be mentioned are in my possession.

ers and barbarously murdered. A lady tied up in her own house, and so forced to witness the murder of her husband. An officer, to save his wife and child from dishonour and abuse, shot them both, before being himself cut down. The massacre at Cawnpore perpetrated by bazaar butchers employed for the purpose. A young lady with her own hand killing five of her assailants, then throwing herself upon her sword rather than fall into the hands of their fellows. A lady, with her husband and child, while endeavouring to escape on horseback; her husband dying in the jungle as a result of exposure; she forced to abandon his corpse, and with her child continue their flight. And so on.

At Berhampore, the 11th Irregular Cavalry and 63rd Native Infantry had recently been disarmed; their horses and arms collected around the military hospital; that building put into a state of defence; houses in its vicinity in process of destruction; guns and other arms being sent into the station by the *Nawab* of Moorshedabad.

At Rajmahal news received that mutineers besieging Arrah had been dispersed; that "something" had happened to a party of the 10th. Havelock's force, in its advance on Lucknow, severely seized by cholera; losses by death,[9] and inefficiency by sickness so great that he was under the necessity of returning to Cawnpore, there to dispose of sick, and obtain reinforcements preparatory to resuming his advance. Sorties by the rebels in Delhi repulsed with heavy loss to them; Lord Elgin arrived at Calcutta, accompanied by some marines and artillery; other reinforcements expected to arrive in a few days.

At Bhaugulpore the display of the Union Jack from a Mahomedan mosque indicated the fact that the edifice was occupied by British troops.[10] We learned also that a portion of the 5th Irregular Cavalry, suspected of mutinous intentions, were about to be disbanded by the 90th Regiment in progress up country; that a few days previous men of the former corps, occupying a

9. Five officers died in one day.

10. A detachment of 5th Fusiliers

station in near vicinity of this place, murdered Sir Norman Leslie, one of their officers, and wounded several others; that, notwithstanding these circumstances, the officer in command urged his confidence in the loyalty of his men, as a reason that they should be spared from the disgrace of being disarmed. His prayer was acceded to. That night the men deserted their officers, rode off with their horses to join the 32nd Native Infantry, at Deoghur.

Monghyr was in a state of panic; a small body of the Northumberland Fusiliers, aided by residents, doing their best to put the dilapidated fort in a state of defence, and making other preparations against possible emergency.

Communication with Agra and Delhi only practicable *via* Bombay; all direct telegraph wires destroyed; military and residents at the first-named place, secure within the fort, declaring themselves able "to hold out" for a long time, notwithstanding that in a *sortie* against the rebels they had suffered severely; at Delhi offensive measures against mutineers languishing by reason of heavy sickness and mortality among our troops besieging that city.

Rejoining the 10th[11] at Dinapore, that station was seen to be without sepoy troops; the barracks formerly occupied by them deserted; the barrack square filled with refugees from neighbouring places. Next day the 90th Regiment, in progress up country, was temporarily detained, as attack by mutineers was anticipated and had to be guarded against; a considerable number of the men fallen sick, had on that account to be landed, for they also were being conveyed by river. A few days thereafter a detachment of the 10th arrived from Jugdispore, at which place they inflicted considerable loss upon the mutineers, who had taken part in the disaster to be presently noticed as having befallen a portion of the regiment at Arrah. But continuity demands some particulars relating to events which led up to the disaster and expedition so alluded to.

---

11. August 18.

144

CHAPTER 13

1857. Early Months of Sepoy Mutiny

The force stationed at Dinapore consisted of two troops of European Artillery, 10th Foot, a portion of the 37th British, the 7th, 8th, and 40th Native Regiments. Among the three last named signs of disaffection had for some time past been apparent to their officers, though unhappily ignored by the general,[1] an old, infirm, and irresolute man. On the 25th of July he was so far moved to action as to direct that percussion caps should be taken away from their magazines of arms, and from the men themselves. A parade for the latter purpose was ordered; thereupon the *sepoys* became openly mutinous, fired upon and otherwise threatened their officers; they finally broke away, taking their arms with them.

Meanwhile, the white troops were not permitted by the general to open fire upon or pursue the mutineers, who, taking the direction of Arrah, soon placed themselves under the leadership of the powerful chief Koer Singh. Arrived at that place, they laid siege to the house of Mr. Boyle, in which the few residents of the small station had collected, and, to some extent, fortified the building.

On the 27th a party consisting of men of the 10th and 37th proceeded by steamer, in view to relief of those besieged; but the vessel ran aground, and so their object was frustrated, On the 29th a second steamer having been procured, the combined party proceeded in her; in due time arrived at Beharee Ghat

1. Lloyd.

145

on the river Sone; there landed, and began their march towards Arrah. Unhappily, a night advance was determined upon. After much toil, not acquainted with the ground, not knowing their way, having to cross a deep ravine or *nullah*, and to surmount other difficulties, they entered the town about midnight, and after the moon had set.

A heavy fire was thereupon opened on them. Men and officers were unable to see each other. Captain Dunbar, the officer in command, fell dead; confusion was the immediate result. A certain number found their way back to the open country; but so heavy were the losses, so great the disorganization of the whole, that the expedition not only failed in its intended object, but met with serious disaster. The remnants were brought back to Dinapore, where they arrived on 30th of July; it was then found that out of 415 officers and men who had started on that service, 170 were killed and 120 wounded, making a total of 290.[2]

The wounded who were rescued were more in number than could be accommodated in hospital; supplementary buildings had accordingly to be utilised for them. Throughout the regiment chagrin and disappointment were general; stories circulated that acts of atrocity had been perpetrated on some of the wounded. Soldiers were loud in their imprecations against the rebels, declaring their determination "to pay them off for it."

Major Eyre, hearing of the disaster that had befallen the troops under Captain Dunbar, advanced by forced marches from Buxar; on August 2 he attacked and dispersed the besieging rebels at Arrah, who thereupon fled towards Jugdispore. On the 8th a party of the 10th under Captain Patterson, together with some other troops, arrived at Arrah from Dinapore. On the nth, in conjunction with those of Major Eyre, it started in pursuit of the *sepoys*; they had taken up a position at a village named Jota Narainpore. There they were attacked by the men of the 10th, who rushed upon them with a shout, killing numbers and dispersing those who escaped their bayonets.

At Dinapore, Sir James Outram inspected the 10th, and hav-

---

2. Out of fifteen officers, twelve were killed or wounded.

ing issued orders with regard to further proceedings continued his journey southwards, taking with him some officers belonging to the mutinous native corps. The arrival of Sir Colin Campbell at Calcutta to assume supreme command was followed by the departure of Sir Patrick Grant to resume his own proper command at Madras. At Patna a partial outbreak by the Mahomedans had recently taken place, Dr. Lyell being killed during it. A recurrence of that disturbance being threatened, a detachment of the 10th was sent to Bankipore as a personal guard to the Commissioner of Behar, whose residence was at that place.

When the great body of the *sepoys* at Dinapore mutinied and fled, certain of their number were employed on various duties within the barrack ranges occupied by the British troops. Unable like their brethren to effect their escape, they laid down their arms, declaring themselves to be loyal, or "staunch," according to the phrase of the day; tents were issued for their use, and a neat little encampment established on a space of open ground between the barracks and adjoining river bank.

In the course of the following night screams issued from that encampment; in due time some soldiers, with their officers, proceeded with lights to the tents, to find several of the *sepoys* dead, others more or less severely wounded by bayonet thrusts, but without any clue to their assailants. Whether or not, as asserted at the time, the men of the 10th were implicated in this dastardly outrage, remained uncleared up by the official inquiry which followed in due course.

In rapid succession news reached us of events at different places within the sphere of mutiny. The investment of Delhi more closely pressed by the combined British and Sikh besieging forces. From Agra that the rebels had withdrawn therefrom. From Oude that Havelock had resumed his advance towards Lucknow, inflicting *en route* severe defeat upon the opposing rebels. From Calcutta that reinforcements were being daily dispatched inland by bullock trains; but as the rate of progress of those animals did not exceed two and a half miles per hour, considerable time must elapse before the troops so sent can be brought into actual use.

Other items of intelligence were, that a body of Ghoorkas sent by Jung Bahadur as an auxiliary force had been attacked by the rebels, upon whom they inflicted defeat with heavy loss. The river steamer *Jumna* in its progress upwards beyond Allahabad was so heavily fired upon by the mutineers, at the same time the water of the Ganges becoming so shallow, that it had to abandon further attempts to proceed; there was therefore no alternative but to withdraw.

In the city of Patna the condition of things, already unsatisfactory, became still more so, the intention of the Mahomedans therein declared to be an attack on the "Kaffirs" on their great festival day of the Mohurrum,[3] falling this year on 31st of August. As a precautionary measure, therefore, a line of defences was rapidly thrown up between the city and cantonments. Next came a report that the 9th Irregular Cavalry, after doing good service at Delhi, had fraternised with the rebels; with them made a dash at a besieging battery protected by Sikhs, their attempt defeated by the 75th Regiment. Then sad accounts of sickness and mortality by disease in addition to casualties in battle among the besiegers; for example, the 1st Battalion 60th Rifles, 400 strong when it first took up its position, had not in its ranks now 200 effectives. From Allahabad the statement came that some of the "staunch" gun *lascars* were detected in an attempt to load their guns with bricks and mortar.

The state of things in our regimental hospital, characteristic of the time, was this:—

In the months of July and August deaths included two officers and seventy men. The long corridor-like wards of the building, together with its veranda, were filled partly with wounded men, remnants of the unfortunate Arrah expedition, partly by those affected with diseases special to the season of the year. The requirements of the wounded demanded much manual attention. What, therefore, between

3. Mohurrum. The first ten days of the Mahomedan New Year are dedicated to the festival so called.

handling wounded tissues and their dressings, finger-tips became sodden like those of a washerwoman, and tender to the touch; the stooping attitude necessary while performing dressings and operations so fatigued the muscles of the back as to make it painful to be in, or again to change that attitude; at the same time the moist heat prevailing made such exertions particularly exhausting. The hospital had already been fortified, arms issued, and so arranged that in case of necessity they could be made use of by some of the patients; sandbags were arranged for purposes of defence on the roof, the walls loop-holed; indeed, the only shots at the escaping *sepoys* of the 40th Native Infantry were from it.

Rumours circulated that a combined line of action by the disaffected in Patna and mutinous *sepoys* under Koer Singh, one of the Nana's lieutenants, was contemplated against Dinapore, garrisoned as the station by only a portion of the 10th Foot. To meet such a contingency, it was proposed to arm the women belonging to the regiment; nor had those of us who had some knowledge of their general style and prowess any doubt as to the result, should they come in conflict with such adversaries. Indeed, there was every reason to believe that already a mutineer had lost his life by the hand of one of our Amazons armed with a bayonet.

The arrival of a Madras infantry regiment, in the ranks of which were some Hindostanees, gave rise to some little speculation as to possible events, should they be brought against their rebel countrymen. At the same time news circulated that a mutinous spirit had been shown in one of the cavalry regiments (8th) of that presidency, and in at least two of infantry (21st and 27th) in that of Bombay.

Under the circumstances of the time, welcome was intelligence by English mail that a powerful force was in progress of dispatch to India; its numerical strength 25,000 men, including Royal Artillery, then to be employed in Hindostan for the first time. Now also came the first faint rumour that the transfer of

149

Indian administration directly to the Government of Her Majesty was intended.

From Meean Meer came news of successful action against intended "rising" on the part of native troops at that station, the attending circumstances of that action being in some respects like those of the historical ball[4] at Brussels on the eve of Quatre Bras. Among the regiments disarmed, as an outcome of that action, was the 26th Native Infantry For some time thereafter the *sepoys* belonging to it remained "loyal" and "contrite."

Suddenly, under the shelter of night,[5] they fled, having first murdered one of their officers. At break of day troops were sent in pursuit; the fugitives overtaken on the left bank of the Ravee. Of their number fully 100 were shot down, 150 or so drowned in their endeavour to swim across that river, the remaining 200 ultimately captured, brought back to their station, and executed. It was of the concluding act of the drama that news now reached us.

In the afternoon of September 4, the *River Bird* arrived from Calcutta, having on board the "Shannon Naval Brigade," under Captain—soon to become Sir William Peel. No sooner were they disembarked than all paraded for drill. Lookers-on rapidly collected to witness the novel proceedings, the wild rollicking manner in which the bluejackets pulled about and worked their ship's guns of large calibre. That evening the officers were our guests at the regimental mess. Our next meeting was to be under circumstances even more stirring than those now taking place.

From time to time the papers of the day gave what statistics were available in regard to lives sacrificed, directly and indirectly, by the present outbreak of the *sepoys*. According to one paper,[6] those numbers were as follows, soldiers, officers, women, and children being included in the totals; namely, Meerut, twenty-nine; Loodianah, three; Sealkote, eight; Fyzabad, seven; Gwalior, fifteen; Rohnee, one; Jounpore, one; Jhelum, one; Allahabad,

---

4. At Meean Meer the ball by the 81st Regiment took place on May 12.
5. July 30.
6. *Phoenix*, September 28, 1857.

fifteen; Mehidpore, seven; Mosuffernuggar, one; Bareilly, seventy; Delhi—on the outbreak of the mutiny, eighty-two,—killed or died by exposure subsequently, forty; Hissar, nine; Shahjehanpore, one; Cawnpore, nineteen (exclusive of those to be subsequently enumerated); Meean Meer, two; Mhow, thirty-four; Sooltanpore, three; Saugur, one; Neemuch, four; Indore, two; Patna, one; Moradabad, four; Darjeeling, one; Futtehpore, one; Lucknow, twenty-two; Benares, five; Agra, sixteen; Jhansi, forty-three; Jullundhur, four; Ferozepore, three; Raneegunge, three; Indore, fifteen; making in all a total of 494.

These numbers do not include the many instances in which lives were sacrificed by exposure and hardship, nor the numerous young soldiers who succumbed while being conveyed along the Grand Trunk Road.

With regard to the most terrible of all episodes,—namely, that of June 27, at Cawnpore,—an account by one of the very few survivors was published in the *Friend of India;* [7] namely,

"Those who in the boats survived from the artillery fire directed upon them were taken back to Cawnpore; the men secured by cords, and with the ladies brought before the Nana, who thereupon gave orders for their destruction. The ladies were placed on one side, the men, bound as they were, drawn up in line, and his troops ordered to fire upon them. Some of the ladies broke away, and rushing to their husbands, clasped them in despair, determined to die with them.

A chaplain who was of the doomed number begged that a few minutes might be granted them to prepare to meet their God—a favour which was granted; others called upon their executioners to finish their bloody work. A volley of musketry; the victims reeled and fell, some dead, others still alive, though wounded; their murderers rush upon them with *tulwars*; [8] they deal death around, nor do they cease their work when life is extinct, but continue to mutilate the bodies of the dead.

The women and children, numbering one hundred and fifty-

---

7. Of September 3, 1857.
8. Native swords.

nine persons, were retained till July 15, and then destroyed by butchers employed for that diabolical purpose. Two days thereafter, but too late to avert the catastrophe the forces led by Havelock entered Cawnpore."

At a somewhat later date further particulars appeared[9] with reference to the same sad episode. According to them the list of persons whose lives were sacrificed there, whether in the entrenchments between June 5 to 27, in the boats on the latter date, or on July 15, when the last remnant was butchered, as just related, was as follows; namely, Honourable Company's Artillery, sixty-one; H.M.'s 32nd Regiment, eighty-four; 1st European Fusiliers, fifteen; H.M.'s 84th Regiment, fifty; officers of regiments and staff, one hundred; merchants, writers, and others, one hundred; drummers, etc., forty; women and children of soldiers, about 160; of writers merchants, and drummers, 120; ladies and children of officers, fifty; servants (after many had absconded early in the outbreak), 100; *sepoys* and native officers sick in hospital, twenty; total, 900. But there is every reason to believe that these figures are approximate rather than actually exact.

Orders were received and quickly carried into effect, whereby the wives and children of men and officers of the 10th were dispatched by steamer to Berhampore, at the time considered a place of safety. A company of our regiment marched towards Gya, then threatened by the mutinous 5th Irregulars, and defended only by a small body of Rattray's Sikhs. The withdrawal of the Treasury from that station resulted in the official ruin of the civilian concerned; but under the circumstances of the time the verdict of opinion among those on the spot was that his action was justified.

Among the refugees proceeding by steamer down country was Mrs. Mills, whose husband, Major Mills, of the Bengal Artillery, had been shot by his mutinous men while endeavouring to escape from Fyzabad, by swimming the Gogra. This unfortunate lady had been wandering in the jungle for nearly three months. She now was ill from hardships and starvation; one child, an

9. *Calcutta Englishman,* October 15, 1857.

infant, had died, the remaining two were ill with cholera; she herself nearly devoid of clothing, without servant or other help, almost completely broken down; nor was it until a few days ago that she learned the fate of her husband.

A brother officer of Major Mills, Captain Alexander, placed a suite of rooms in his house at her disposal. In due time she and her children were so far restored in health, and provided with clothing, that they continued their journey towards Calcutta.

For sometime past a detachment of the 5th Fusiliers occupied a building connected with the Opium Stores in Patna, the rate of sickness and mortality among the men composing it being so great as to equal 90 *per cent*, of deaths per 100 strength *per annum*. A visit to the place by Colonel Fenwick and myself revealed the fact that the quarters assigned to them were in all respects unsuited; while, therefore, the remaining portion of the men were withdrawn, their place taken by men of the 10th, steps were taken, and successfully, to avert similar casualties among the latter.

Still there came news of mutiny from stations far apart: from Assam on the one hand, to Ferozepore on the other; while of regiments of the Bombay Presidency, a similar spirit had extended to at least four of their number. Indeed, so general had mutiny become that scarcely a remark was made as the news of some fresh outbreak circulated; but among officers and men of our regiment the desire was loudly expressed to "get fairly at them in the field," little if any account being taken of relative numbers.

At this time my own physical state gave way under the weight of arduous duties; several brother officers also were rendered temporarily incapable of work; but at the earliest possible date we returned to our respective spheres, determined to "put the shoulder to the wheel." The good news reached us that a further defeat had been inflicted upon the Arrah mutineers by Major Eyre. The arrival of reinforcements by ship from England had begun to cause wonder and some consternation among the rebels. For reasons the nature of which did not transpire, certain newspapers were temporarily suppressed.

The immediate result of that measure was that private letters took the place of the journals so dealt with; groups of men assembled at the post office on the occasion of morning delivery, news was interchanged, and thus a tolerable knowledge maintained of events in progress at different stations.

From Azimghur came information that there the rebels had been attacked and defeated by the Ghoorka troops of Jung Bahadur.[10] It was said that a force consisting of 3,000 Cashmere troops, sent by Goolab Singh, was approaching Delhi, in aid of the British, by whom the siege of that city was being vigorously pressed on.

Then came news that on September 16 an entrance had been effected by the Cashmere Gate; 125 guns captured, though with a loss to our troops engaged of between forty and fifty officers and 650 men killed and wounded. From Nagpore, that the mutinous 50th Native Infantry had been attacked, and to a great extent destroyed by the column advancing from Madras. From the Punjab, that some fifty men of the 10th Cavalry and a number of mutineers of the 55th Native Infantry had been executed by order of Sir John Lawrence. In contrast with these energetic measures were Proclamations by Government, full of sympathetic expressions with regard to "the poor misguided men," as applied to the perpetrators of deeds already alluded to.

A few days passed, and then came information that very stirring events were in progress; that Delhi was completely in the hands of our troops, the king a prisoner, two royal princes shot by the hand of Hodson.[11] The forces under Havelock and Outram had effected [12] an entrance into the Residency of Lucknow, and so "relieved" the besieged garrison of that city. The story of that "relief" was everywhere related with pride. But the fact was deplored that the "relieving" force, as a result of the losses sustained, had itself to add its numbers to the besieged. Among the

---

10. At Manduri, ten miles from that station.
11. On September 21, 1857.
12. On September 25, 1857

latter, casualties by shot and disease had, up to the date of "relief," included fifty-seven women and children.

On the following Sunday, collections were made in cantonment churches, for the purposes of a fund being raised wherewith to aid sufferers by the present rebellion.

Thereafter news of successes at different points against the rebels came in rapidly. Thus from Delhi a force had gone in pursuit of one party of them; in Central India the 52nd Native Infantry was broken up by the Madras column; near Sherghotty the Ramghur Battalion annihilated; in the vicinity of Mirzapore a body of mutineers defeated by a small force comprising the 5th Fusiliers and 17th Madras Native Infantry

At this time the "Pearl" Brigade, under command of Captain Sotheby, arrived at Dinapore; two companies of the 10th, under Major Longden, started towards Benares, there to be ready for emergencies. At intervals disaffection occurred in portions of the 32nd Native Infantry, occupying various positions in neighbouring districts. Now came news that the last fragment of that corps had broken into mutiny and fled; their object to unite with the rebel force beyond the Soane, commanded by Koer Singh.

Information was received that a body of mutineers 4,000 strong, with twelve guns, was in progress from Oude to make an attack on the Treasury at Chupra, and afterwards to threaten our small body of effectives at Dinapore. Then we learned that Rajah Maun Singh, of Gorruckpore, hitherto believed to be "loyal,"— he having given protection to some ladies whose husbands had been murdered by the *sepoys*,—had joined the rebels with a force of 9,000 men.

As a counterpoise to such items, the troops under Colonel Greathead, descending by the Grand Trunk Road, had defeated the *sepoys*, inflicting heavy loss upon them, subsequently possessing himself of Alighur, together with its guns and stores. A significant indication of the tendency now being assumed by bazaar opinion was that native bankers, who in the first outbreak of the mutiny sent their treasure to Calcutta, are having it brought back to their places of business.

We were at this time in a position to estimate the strength of reinforcements already sent, and in process of being dispatched from England, to re-establish authority in India. These comprised eleven regiments of Light Cavalry; fifty-five battalions of Infantry; four troops of Horse Artillery; eleven companies of Foot Artillery; seven Field Batteries; four companies of Engineers, equal to a total of 87,000 men. With these there were fourteen medical officers, over and above those pertaining to regiments and other bodies.

As each successive body of troops arrived, officers belonging to them were invited to our mess; thus we gathered something in regard to the tenor of opinion in England in reference to events in progress around us. Very different was the impression so conveyed, of views entertained at home, from what under the actual circumstances of the time was to be expected. From the long distance, the *sepoy* was looked upon as mild and harmless in disposition, but driven to revolt by acts of oppression to which he had been long subjected,—those acts, however,! not definitely stated; Sir John Lawrence and General Neil were said to be cruel and otherwise objectionable persons; the policy of "clemency" all that was estimable, and to be desired. The contrast between the views so expressed, and actual occurrences such as have been already mentioned, taking place almost before our very eyes, gave rise to comments, some of them more expressive than sympathetic.

Meanwhile the progress of events went on. A body of mutinous *sepoys* had found their way from Delhi to Bithoor, the residence of the Nana. There they were attacked by a force sent for the purpose from Cawnpore, under the command of Colonel Wilson, their stronghold destroyed, guns, ammunition, and other stores contained in it captured. At Raneegunge the Headquarter portion of the 32nd Native Infantry[13] was disarmed by Colonel Burney, their commanding officer, to whom was given up also the treasonable correspondence being carried on by the *sepoys* belonging to it.

13. From Deoghur.

At Agra the camp was attacked by a body of rebel cavalry, estimated at 1,500 strong. The picquet of the 9th Lancers, comprising not more than twenty-four troopers, under command of Captain French and Lieutenant Jones, charged and cut its way through them; but in so doing the first-named officer was killed, the second wounded. The station of Chupra in our near vicinity being threatened, the "Pearl" Brigade, under Captain Sotheby, R.N., was ordered by the Civil Commissioner of Patna to proceed for its protection—a new experience for a naval officer to be ordered by a civilian. At our own station reinforcements, comprising a portion of the 82nd Regiment, were a welcome addition to our weak garrison. Particulars were published of the cost in casualties at which the troops under Havelock attained the relief of the Lucknow garrison; namely, sixteen officers killed and forty-five wounded; of soldiers, 400 killed and 700 wounded, equal to nearly one-third of the force engaged. No wonder that in their turn the remnants became part of the besieged garrison.

The party of the 10th already at Benares was held in readiness to enter Oude, and there act as occasion might require against assemblages of mutineers. At Jounpore, a body of rebels were attacked by the Ghoorkas, who severely defeated them, killing or disabling some 250 out of 1,200 of their strength. Some ghastly indications of events in progress were furnished by floating bodies in the Ganges, these being seen during several successive days, as with vultures or other foul birds perched upon and tearing their flesh they were carried past our station. Among them were six white bodies, lashed together by ropes, suggesting the means by which the victims had been destroyed.

By the end of October, Sir Colin Campbell started from Calcutta to assume direct command of the troops actively engaged against the enemy. Travelling by "*dâk*," and having with him an escort of inconsiderable strength, he narrowly escaped capture by the mutineers of the 32nd Native Infantry, who lay in wait in the vicinity of the Soane, his escape being due to the fleetness of his "*gharry*" horses. After that incident the same party of mutineers doubled back and endeavoured to enter Oude by crossing the Ganges near Patna, but were defeated in their attempt by the armed river steamer *Koladyne* (See note following).

Note—

Forty years thereafter,—namely, in 1897,—Lord Roberts, bearing in mind the events of 1857, writes:—In reply to the question, "Is there any chance of a mutiny occurring again?"

With reference to that question he remarks after this manner

"I would say that the best way of guarding against such a calamity is—By never allowing the present proportion of British to native soldiers to be diminished or the discipline and efficiency of the native army to become slack.

"By taking care that men are selected for the higher civil and military posts whose self-reliance, activity, and resolution are not impaired by age, and who possess a knowledge of the country and the habits of the peoples.

"By recognising and guarding against the dogmatism of theorists and the dangers of centralization.

"By rendering our administration on the one hand firm and strong, on the other hand tolerant and sympathetic; and last, but not least, by doing all in our power to gain the confidence of the various races, and by convincing them that we have not only the determination, but the ability to maintain our supremacy in India against all assailants.

"If these cardinal points are never lost sight of, there is, I believe, little chance of any fresh outbreak disturbing the stability of our rule in India, or neutralizing our efforts to render that country prosperous, contented, and thoroughly loyal to the British Crown." (Vol. 1., p. 449.)

In bitterly sarcastic terms the policy of "clemency" towards and sympathy expressed for the "misguided" *sepoy* found utterance after this manner in the *Friend of India:*[14]—

---

14. Of November 5, 1857.

Pity the sorrows of a mild Hindoo, whose tottering steps have brought him to your door. To murder you he did what man could do, and can you blame him that he did no more? Ripped from the body of your outraged wife, he tossed your unborn babe upon his pike! Yearns not your heart to save and sooth the life of one who thirsts again to do the like?

You do not kill the serpent in your path, you do not crush the bug when you have caught him; And why bear malice 'gainst one who hath but turned on you the arms whose use you've taught him. Those arms at present I have flung away, finding that somehow we miscalculated; And that we should have picked a luckier day to glut us with the blood we hated. And now I stand expectant at your gate, trusting for pardon and fraternal love:

Of serpent wisdom you have shown of late not much; show me the softness of the dove. And then I promise you, as time shall suit, the rich reward you'll have deserved to share, The untiring hate of a remorseless brute, the poison of the reptile that you spare.

While Peel's *Shannon* Brigade, so recently with us, was in progress from Allahabad to Cawnpore, it became united to the 53rd and a party of the 93rd Regiments. The combined force was seriously engaged at Futtehpore with a strong body of mutineers, and although successful in defeating them severely, after a conflict of two hours' duration, the victory was at the cost of many lives, among them Colonel Powell, formerly a brother officer in the 57th.

The mutineers of the 32nd Native Infantry, unable to cross into Oude, had again taken up a position on the Soane; there they were attacked and defeated by Rattray's Sikhs, though not without severe proportional loss among the latter. The party of the 10th from Benares came in contact with and routed a body of the Oude rebels at Atrowlea. Meanwhile the forces under Sir Colin Campbell were fighting their way from Cawnpore towards Lucknow.

Martial law had for some time past existed at Dinapore. In accordance with that effective code a Court-Martial was ordered to assemble for the trial of a sepoy of 14th Native Infantry, on the charge of taking part in the massacre of our men at Arrah, as already mentioned. Before that tribunal the man was duly tried; by it convicted and sentenced to suffer death by being blown from a gun.

Early in the day following a strong guard of the 10th took charge of the doomed man, to whom, in the usual way, the sentence of the court was read. He was immediately marched to the rear of the barracks, where preparations were complete for carrying into effect the dreadful penalty. His step was firm, though his countenance expressed despair and terror; his hands quivered, lips moved as if in prayer.

While being secured in the fatal position, he seemed dazed; the heart-beat reduced to a mere flutter; a bandage tied over his eyes, he faintly said, *"Hummara kussoor nahin hye"* —it is not my fault. The officiating assistant stood aside, the hand of the Provost Marshal was raised, there was a loud report, and shreds of humanity flew in various directions. A scene to be witnessed only under compunction of circumstances. Mutineer prisoners brought to the station for that purpose had in all cases fair and open trial.

Welcome was the news that" during the night between November 22 and 23 the besieged garrison of Lucknow had been withdrawn therefrom by the force under Sir Colin Campbell, and was being escorted towards Cawnpore. At the same time accounts reached us of the attack by the Gwalior contingent on the last-named station; of their temporary success by reason of numbers, and of their defeat with heavy loss in men and guns by the commander-in-chief. Worn out by fatigue,—for he was physically a delicate man,—General Havelock fell a victim to cholera shortly after reaching the outskirts of Lucknow.

In the vicinity of Jounpore a small British force came in contact with the Oude rebels. On that occasion our Ghoorka allies were said to have expressed a wish not to fight any more, and to have shown their reluctance accordingly. Then came information that a large number of ladies and children from those besieged, together with a considerable body of sick and wounded soldiers, had arrived safely at Allahabad from Cawnpore, *en route* to Calcutta.

Chapter 14

1857–1858. The Jounpore Field Force

Orders to take the field had been expected, and preparations made accordingly in the 10th, so that when they did arrive all was in readiness to carry them out immediately. Uncertainty for some time prevailed with respect to the 73rd Native Infantry, professedly and somewhat demonstratively "loyal," but known to be in a dangerous state of disaffection, ready to sweep over the indigo-yielding places in Tirhoot, some of the planters from which, abandoning houses and factories, had betaken themselves to Dinapore for safety.

A report spread that a body of rebels had crossed the river Gogra and threatened the *Pearl* Brigade at Sewan; a steamer accordingly started to Benares, conveying detachments of the 10th and 37th Regiments, to be in readiness to act from that base as circumstances might require. Reports at the same time told that the nth Irregulars had broken away from Berhampore; that they had been severely handled by the 5th Fusiliers, but that they were making their way towards Tirhoot.

By daylight on December 23, a detachment of our men and officers was in progress of embarking on board a steamer for conveyance towards Chuprah, at and from which place they were intended to act in concert with bodies of Ghoorka troops for the assistance of threatened stations in Tirhoot. Equally early on the 24th our headquarters marched away from barracks. Arriving in due time at the point where the Ganges was to be crossed, much delay resulted from the incompleteness of arrangements made for the purpose.

Evening had far advanced when we arrived on our camping-ground; tents were far behind; so were the messing arrangements. From such "reserves "as our haversacks supplied our first meal was taken, after which we bivouacked "on the cold ground," under shelter of a mango grove. Next day being Christmas Day, equipment and arrangements were got into working order and ready for eventualities.

On the 26th the sound of firing, as if at Sewan, indicated that the arrival of the 10th was none too soon, and shortly thereafter news came in that an attack, not determined in character, by the mutineers had been repulsed. In the course of the next few days the Nepaulese contingent captured a considerable number of mutineers belonging to the nth Irregulars, but those of the 5th Irregulars succeeded in joining the body of rebels assembled under Koer Singh.

New Year's Day brought the welcome news that the rebels had been severely beaten at Alumbagh by Sir James Outram, great loss inflicted upon them, and four of their guns captured; also that Colonel Seton had defeated a body of mutineers at Futtyghur. Having moved our camp to a position north-westward of the town, we discovered a saltpetre manufactory for the use of the rebels. Firing was again heard in our near vicinity, indicative, as we soon learned, that our Nepaulese allies had attacked a rebel village, which they captured and destroyed.

The 10th were ordered to advance towards Azimghur, to be joined en route by other regiments, the combined force to be named the Jounpore Field Force, commanded by Brigadier-General Franks. On the second day of our progress, at a place called Muttyala, the first active signs of disaffection were shown by some of the villagers; it was quickly suppressed, however, by the simple method of handing over to the Provost Marshal those who had so acted, and having them flogged.

No further trouble with natives was experienced; and so, without adventure, on the fourth day of our march we crossed the river Gogra, and entered the district of Azimghur. Thence to the provincial city our progress was cautious and wary; villages through which our route lay were seen to be deserted by their ordinary inhabitants, except the old and very young, by women and the infirm.

At Azimghur—once a pretty and otherwise favoured station—the public buildings, including the church, had been reduced to charred and roofless walls, gardens wasted and disfigured; a series of huts in course of being erected for the faithless *sepoys* at the time, when on June 3 the 17th Native Infantry broke into mutiny, left standing as they then were; the gaol strongly fortified, everything destructible bearing an aspect of ruin. Within the intrenched position at the gaol a small force of Ghoorkas kept at defiance the rebel *sepoys* who had already made two unsuccessful attacks, with considerable loss in life and of two of their guns.

Resuming our progress, the 10th reached Aroul on January 26. There the various portions [1] of the force of which we were to form a part united, and was organized for its prospective duties. A halt of three days sufficed. On the 29th a march of twenty-three miles was performed by our little army, the minimum quantity of equipment and transport accompanying it. Several houses in ruins, belonging to planters, were passed in our progress to the river Goomtee; that river was crossed, and about midnight we bivouacked on Oude territory. By break of day our force was again in motion towards its objective point, now known to be Lucknow. That day's march was uneventful, except that the water in the roadside wells was rendered unpalatable by branches of neem tree (*Melia Azadirachta*) thrown into them by the rebels.

A short halt was made at Singramow, during which preparation was made for eventualities. Intimation was there received that the rebels were collecting their forces at Chanda, about a dozen miles in front of us, and that their pickets had advanced to within four or five miles of our camp. On February 19 our

---

1. Our force consisted of the 10th, 20th, and 97th British regiments; six battalions of Nepaulese troops, under the command of General Pulwan Singh; two Field Batteries, and some thirty to forty mounted men of the 10th. By virtue of seniority I assumed medical charge.

force was under arms at daylight, and then began its advance towards the enemy. About nine o' clock a halt was ordered; men and officers partook of such "breakfast" as under the circumstances they could get, while staff officers rode to the front to reconnoitre.

A long line of rebels was seen to occupy a somewhat elevated position at a little distance from us. Our guns immediately advanced, opened fire upon them, their fire being for a short time returned. The 10th—Colonel Fenwick at their head— threw out their skirmishers, and thus covered, advanced at steady pace towards the point where the rebels seemed thickest. They, however, did not long stand their ground; before our men came within striking distance the *sepoys* gave way and took to flight. Pursuit was impossible, by reason of want of cavalry; but the small band of mounted infantry, recently extemporised from the 10th, managed to come up, with some of the enemy, of whom, in the language of the day, they "gave a good account." We subsequently learned that the forces against whom we had been engaged comprised 8,000 men, commanded by Bunda Hussun, a lieutenant of Mendhee Hussun.

It was intended that our force should encamp on the field whence the rebels had fled. While halting for that purpose, it was found that a second engagement was to take place; that the enemy had taken up a position at Hummeerpore, a little distance from their former, and under shelter of a wood. From there their guns soon opened fire upon us. Ours quickly replied; a few casualties in our ranks were the result, when darkness having put an end to the duel we bivouacked on our ground. When morning dawned, it was seen that the position they had occupied was abandoned; our camp was accordingly pitched, and so we remained, prepared for the next move.

Resuming our advance towards Lucknow, two successive marches of great length, and consequently fatiguing, were performed, considerable numbers of our transport animals completely breaking down, and so being the cause of much inconvenience to our force.

On the 23rd, about 10 a.m., our skirmishers drew upon them fire from a position taken up by the rebels at Sooltanpore. That position was attacked, and from a direction unexpected by them; thus disconcerted, their fire was comparatively little destructive in our ranks, nor was it long before—having discharged upon us a volley of grape—they abandoned their artillery and fled, leaving fourteen guns, besides stores and a large quantity of equipment, in our possession, also much ammunition and loot.

Again the mounted men of the 10th [2] did good service in pursuit of the fugitives; some of our artillery followed, and it was said destroyed large numbers of them, the loss to our troops engaged being again comparatively small. Thus were the forces of Mendhee Hussun defeated, though numbering 6,000 regular *sepoys* and 6,000 matchlock men; the station of Sooltanpore recovered after being held by the rebels since the previous month of June.

After some delay our camp was pitched on the ground our men had won, and we halted for a day. A party dispatched to destroy a manufactory of gun carriages deserted by the rebels came upon various relics, with which doubtless were connected sad and painful associations; these included what had been an elegant *barouche*, a *palkee garree*, and a metal toy—the whole pertaining to victims of the first outburst of mutiny among the troops there stationed. Near our camp the artillery were occupied in bursting the guns deserted by the enemy. On the 25th our force resumed its march at daylight, and so continued till late in the afternoon, making one short halt to allow the troops to draw water from some village wells, a second to cook and distribute food.

Shortly after we had started a very hideous object presented itself to view; it was the body of a native suspended by the feet from a branch of a tree, his arms dangling in midair, and so doubtless indicating the cruel manner of his death. Arrived at Mosufferkhan, where it was arranged that our camp should be pitched, we found awaiting to join us a reinforcement of Sikh

---

2. Under Captain Bartholomew.

and Pathan Horse, together with some mounted men comprising half-castes and Christians who had belonged to mutinied or disbanded regiments all of whom had been sent by forced marches to our aid. Some stray mutineers were discovered in near proximity to camp by our scouts, and by them duly "disposed of."

A long and arduous march through difficult country; the villages along our route deserted by their inhabitants, the fields destitute of labourers. On arrival at our camping ground near Jugdispore, it was ascertained that our advance guard had fallen in with and captured two messengers conveying a *purwana*, or order, from the Ranee of Lucknow to the *zemindars* of the district just traversed by us, intimating to them the advance of a small body of English, and calling upon them to destroy the intruders at Sooltanpore; also to send without delay provisions for the rebel troops holding Lucknow. A day's halt and much-needed rest for man and animal.

On 28th a long march, in the course of which we passed through some villages strongly fortified and loopholed, but deserted by inhabitants. Reinforced as we now were by cavalry, they scoured the vicinity of our route, in the course of their proceedings coming upon seventeen rebels, some wearing the uniform of their former regiments, all of whom they killed.

With rain and boisterous weather the month of March began; it was therefore somewhat late in the morning of the 1st when our advance was resumed. As we proceeded, the discovery was made by our scouts that a considerable body of rebels occupied a point al some little distance on our flank. The main body of our force was accordingly halted, while a portion was sent against the mutineers, the result being that in the attack upon them the latter had sixty of their numbers killed or wounded, and lost two of their guns. Resuming progress, we traversed a number of towns and villages, all strongly fortified, but sparsely occupied. Night had closed in when we reached our halting-place. While tents were being pitched, lurid flames at intervals in our near vicinity told the fate of villages and isolated houses.

During the attack just mentioned several hand-to-hand conflicts took place between the Sikh troopers and the rebels. In one of these an officer received a *tulwar* cut which severed an artery. By-and-by I came upon him, prostrate on the ground, alone, and bleeding to death. A ligature was applied to the divided vessel; he was placed in a *dooly*, and so carried to my tent, where he remained during the following night.

While there he was visited by some of his men, who laid before him various articles of loot—some valuable—of which they had possessed themselves, and now presented to him. In contrast with an incident shortly to be related, and also in its way characteristic of a class, the fact made an impression upon me that under the particular circumstances of time and place, the officer alluded to [3] offered to me—who in all likelihood had been the means of saving his life—not one thing of the many laid out for display on the floor rug of my tent.

Early on March 3 the sound of heavy guns from the direction of Lucknow told that active work was in progress there. Later in the day a staff officer, escorted by a squadron of the 9th Lancers and two Horse Artillery guns, arrived in camp as bearer of dispatches. These contained orders that on the morrow our force should advance and take up the position assigned to it in relation to the contemplated attack on that capital. They informed us that already the Dilkhosha had been captured.

On the following day our force was accordingly in motion towards Lucknow. It had not proceeded far when information was received that a small body of rebels occupied the inconsiderable fort of Dowraha, situated at the distance of a mile or so from our line of route. A body, unfortunately, as events proved, too small for its intended purpose, was detached with the object of effecting its capture; but with the loss of one officer killed and several casualties among the rank and file, the position had to be left untaken, while our force continued its march. In the afternoon we took up the position assigned to us on an extensive plain between Dilkhosha and Bebeepore, and so merged into the general force under the commander-in-chief.

---

3. For his gallantry in the attack mentioned he was awarded the Victoria Cross.

CHAPTER 15

1858. Capture of Lucknow

Throughout March 5 heavy bombardment continued, the batteries of rebels within Lucknow replying actively to those outside the city. On the 6th, Captain Graham's company of the 10th occupied an intrenched position at an angle of the Mohamed Bagh, where during the night temporary defences had been thrown up, the task assigned to, and successfully performed, being by their rifle fire to keep down that from rebel guns of a battery close to Begum Serai.

It became an exciting sight to watch the enemy as they moved their guns into the several embrasures of their battery preparatory to discharging them upon our position, and then the effect of the volley poured into those embrasures by our men; then the burst of flame— our soldiers instantly throwing themselves prone on the ground; the thud of round shot upon our protecting rampart; our soldiers starting to their feet, pouring volley after volley as before into the embrasures, while the guns were being lowered therefrom to be reloaded. Thus the seemingly unequal duel went on. After a time the rebel fire from that particular point began to slacken, then ceased. The men of the 10th had done their work right well. Other portions of our general force were engaged elsewhere, preparatory to the grand attack about to be delivered.

Steadily during the next two days the circle of fire narrowed around the city. On the 9th a more than usual heavy artillery fire took place between our forces and the enemy. The sailors' battery of 68-pounders was engaged against large bodies of the rebels assembled among a range of ruined buildings at the western end of the

Martinière, the men who worked the guns taking affairs with such coolness that, in the intervals between firing, cleaning, and loading their respective pieces, they squatted in parties of four on the ground, and proceeded with games of cards, in which they seemed to take as much interest as in the effect produced by their fire. About 2 p.m., to an increased rapidity, of fire from sailors and artillery guns was added more active *pings* of rifles, and somewhat later on the position of the Martinière was in the possession of our force.

Two more days of arduous work by all ranks, the rebels gradually but steadily being pressed in from their advanced positions; the siege guns opening heavily upon the city; bodies of rebels in their endeavours at flight falling into the hands of our troops, many of their own numbers being killed. Our force increased by the arrival of reinforcements from Cawnpore, and by that of 10,000 Ghoorkas under Jung Bahadur, the advent of the latter causing some interest, and not a little amusement, dirty and untidy, flat-faced, small-sized as they were, their guns drawn by men instead of horses, their whole aspect more suited to dramatic effect than for such work as was then in progress.

On March 11 the Begum Kotee was stormed and captured by a combined force of 93rd Highlanders, 4th Sikhs, and Ghoorkas, the losses sustained by the assailants being on the occasion very heavy in both men and officers. In the afternoon of next day, the 10th, led by Colonel Fenwick, occupied the position thus so gallantly won. Everywhere around signs indicated the deadly nature of the struggle that had taken place during its assault. Bodies of defenders, bleeding and mangled, lay in heaps; some were being thrown pell-mell into a V-shaped ditch, down, then up the sides of which our troops had in the first instance to scramble, while exposed to terrific fire by the defenders.

As we entered, our artillery hastened to prepare for its further work of bombarding at close quarters. During the night we bivouacked within the city. On the 13th, the 10th forced its way against severe opposition directly through the city towards the Kaiser Bagh, while other portions of the troops were similarly

170

at work from other directions. Again, as night closed in after a day of most arduous work and heavy list of casualties among our numbers, the 10th bivouacked in streets and gardens wrested from their sepoy occupants.

On the 14th the regiment went on with its work of conquest, heavy fire from roofs and loopholes bringing to earth, now one, then another, and another of our men as we continued to advance. At last the Kaiser Bagh was reached; it was quickly entered by Captain Annesly at the head of his company, by means of a gateway first detected by Havelock, then adjutant of the 10th; thus the central point within the city, held by the rebels, was now in the hands of our troops.

At a short distance from that position, and partly hidden by other buildings, were the ruins of what had until the previous day been the residence of the notorious Moulvie,[4] by whose orders, in the earlier days of the mutiny, several of our countrymen and countrywomen who had fallen into the hands of the rebels were put to death. As our troops now entered the enclosure within which those ruins stood, they came upon two gory heads of British soldiers, who had during recent operations been captured by the rebels. The Moulvie had, however, escaped, but was known to be in the still unsubdued part of the city, whence he exerted command over the rebels yet actively engaged against our forces.

A communication of romantic and pathetic interest now reached the more advanced portion of our force. It detailed the fact that two ladies [5] were in the hands of the rebels, their lives threatened, their position in other respects one of serious danger; it urged those into whose hands it might fall to press onwards to their rescue. As subsequently transpired, those ladies were held prisoners by Wajid Ali, and by him treated with some degree of consideration, so much so that suspicion was brought upon him

---

4. The Moulvie of Fyzabad, known by the name of Ahmed Alee Shah (also called Ahmed Oola Shah), was a native of Arcot, in the Madras Presidency. He was said to understand English and to have been a man of acumen and boldness. He was ultimately killed at Powayne.

5. Mrs. Orr and Miss Jackson.

in respect to his fidelity to the rebel cause. He it was also who sent, by the hand of his brother, to the nearest British officer, the letter alluded to. Instantly on receipt of it, Captain McNeil and Lieutenant Bogle, at the head of a rescue party of Ghoorkas, started under the guidance of the bearer of the letter. The house in which the ladies were was quickly reached; the two captives were placed in *doolies*, and together with their protector escorted, notwithout much difficulty and risk, to the camp of General Macgregor.

While these operations were in progress, one or other regimental surgeon was constantly with the fighting line, rendering what aid was practicable to those struck down; and here it is well to mention that whenever officer or soldier felt himself wounded, his first call was "for the doctor." Nor is it to be questioned that' the moral effect of our presence was very considerable; the presence of a hand to succour imparted confidence.

As soon as practicable, the wounded were withdrawn to our hospital tents, and there their injuries more particularly attended to. While work in front was in progress, and as a consequence that in hospital was most active, I was on an occasion occupied during twilight in so affording aid to a wounded soldier just brought in, myself on my knees on the ground and leaning over him.

A touch on my shoulder, and then in a soldier's voice, "Here, sir, put that in your haversack," the action accompanying the word, and the man passed on his way, my attention too much occupied to observe his appearance. When work was done and I returned to my tent, I examined my haversack; I found therein a brick of silver, of sufficient size to make, as subsequently it did, a tea and coffee service, the donor remaining unknown. The circumstance is noted, as in contrast to that already mentioned, in which an officer was concerned.

A visit to the Martinière revealed the effects of recent operations against that building; statues and other works of art dilapidated, broken, and in ruins; doors and other woodwork torn and split, walls, ceilings, corridors injured in every possible way, large masses of *débris* at particular places indicating those upon which shot and shell had been most heavily directed. From the summit of the building we traced the route by which, in the previous October, the relieving force had effected its advance, together .with some of the buildings historically associated .with that gallant feat, including the Yellow House, Secundra Bagh, Mess House, and Motee Mahal.

In our field hospital the wreck of our "glorious victory" was to be seen in plenty; officers and soldiers, wounded, maimed, or in various instances terribly burnt and disfigured by explosions; many groaning in their agony, others placidly bearing their sufferings, a few unconscious to pain, the death-rattle in their throats— all arranged on pallets, and far less comfortably seen to than were their comrades fortunate enough to be taken into their own regimental hospitals.

The streets along which the 10th had so recently forced its way to the Kaiser Bagh presented a scene of utter devastation: walls blackened, loopholed, shattered with shot-holes of various sizes, the buildings roofless and tenantless except by dead bodies gashed or torn by bullets, their cotton-wadded clothing burning, sickening odours therefrom contaminating the air; heaps of *débris* everywhere, furniture, utensils and dead bodies, all mixed up together; breaches made by heavy guns to make way for advancing infantry, round shot by which they had been effected; domes, at one time gilded and otherwise ornamental, but now dilapidated and charred; costly furniture, oil paintings once of great value, ornamental glass and china strewed about, and everywhere to be seen; ornamental garden lakes black from gunpowder cast into them; the gardens trodden down, mosaic work of cisterns broken into fragments. At Secundra Bagh, where on November 16 some two thousand *sepoys* perished at the hands of the 53rd and 93rd Regiments, the bones of the slain, now, four months after the event, lay in heaps, a heavy odour of decomposition pervading the enclosure.

At the Residency a deep irregular-shaped pit immediately outside the Bailee Guard marked the spot where, in the latter days of the memorable siege, the rebels had prepared their mine against the defenders of that position; inside and close to the same entrance were the remains of the countermine by which the operations connected with the former were detected, and itself sprung upon the besiegers.

The door of that gateway, penetrated and torn by bullets; buildings roofless and bespattered with shot-marks, including that where ladies and children spent the eighty-five days to which the siege extended, and that in which Sir Henry Lawrence received his death-wound,—the whole presenting an epitome of what war implies, not to be forgotten.

For some time after Lucknow was virtually in the power of our force desultory fights continued to occur at places in and around the city. In the portions actually held by our troops, isolated men occasionally fell by a rebel bullet. Among other casualties, two officers had the misfortune to fall into the hands of the *sepoys*, by whom they were put to death, and their heads, so report said, borne away as trophies.

No sooner had the principal positions held by the rebels been captured from them than their flight from the city began, at first in small bodies, but rapidly increasing in numbers as channels of egress became known among them. Although without artillery, considerable numbers carried their small arms, while others were content to abandon everything, and seek only their own safety.

One armed body of the fugitives, while endeavouring to get away in the direction of the Alumbagh, was fallen upon by our troops and severely dealt with; in other directions, however, the fact became known that large bodies effected their escape without being attacked, in places where no special difficulties intervened,—nor did explanation of the circumstance transpire.

Several field columns were immediately organized and dispatched along different routes known or believed to have been taken by the escaped rebels. Years afterwards the gallant services performed by one of those columns [6] were detailed in a published Biography. Other bodies found their way to the neighbourhood

---

6. Sir Hope Grant, K.C.B.

of Azimghur and there united with a considerable force of their brethren, which had on March 21 defeated a small body of British troops at Atrowlea, obliging it to retire within entrenchments at the first-named city.

CHAPTER 16

1858. The Azimghur Field Force

The task of the 10th was looked upon as finished; the regiment had been sixteen years in India, the entire period continuously in the plains. With an expression of glee on the part of
the men was the order received to commence our homeward
march,—that is, to proceed towards Calcutta, there to embark
for England. On the 28th of March the regiment turned its back
on Lucknow; after several hours of weary progress it reached its
camping ground. About midnight we were roused from slumber
by the arrival of a cavalry escort and staff officer, with orders
that the regiment should march forthwith towards Goorsagunge,
there to form part of a field force under command of Brigadier-
General Lugard, its object to raise what had become the siege of
Azimghur by the combined rebel forces just mentioned.

Before ten o' clock on the 29th our soldiers, to use their own
expression, had "done twenty-eight miles of road, heel and toe,"
disappointed at the unexpected change in destination, but also,
in their own phrase, "ready for the new work cut out for them."
Other portions of what was to be the Azimghur Field Force[1]
quickly reached the appointed rendezvous, and the process of
organization was complete. Then we learned that the combined
rebel force under Koer Singh surrounded Azimghur; that a body
of British, while *en route* thither from Benares, had suffered se-

---

1. It comprised 10th, 34th, and 84th Regiments, 1,700 Sikh cavalry, a portion of
military train as cavalry, and three batteries of artillery. I was principal medical officer, also in charge of the Staff, in addition to my regimental duties.

verely while in conflict with them; that therefore the rapid advance of that under General Lugard was urgently called for.

Continuing our march from day to day, we traversed much of the route by which our advance upon Lucknow had recently lain, it being marked by whitened bones of men slain, ruins of villages, and huts destroyed by fire; otherwise no event worth notice occurred until the 9th of April, by which date we had reached Budlapore. On the morning of that day our force marched from its camp at 2 a.m., proceeding thence direct to Jounpore, a distance of twenty miles. There information was received that the rebel troops around Azimghur were commanded by Mendhee Hussun, Koer Singh being present with them.

Men and animals, tired out by fatiguing marches, were equally constrained to make one day's halt. On the morning of the 11th information led General Lugard to deviate from the regular route and proceed towards Tigra, situated on our left, adjoining the left side of the river Goomtee, the rebels under Gholam Hussun being reported to have there taken up a position. A reconnoitring party speedily discovered the point taken up by about 500 rebels with two guns; they were at once attacked by our irregular cavalry, eighty of their number killed, the remainder dispersed, though this small affair lost the life of Lieutenant Havelock, cousin of our Adjutant.

Another day's halt to rest our men and animals; the heat already severe, 102^0 F. in our tents. Resuming our progress, our force arrived within striking distance of Azimghur after darkness of the night had closed in, and bivouacked on the position assigned to us, the rebels for some time disturbing our rest by their bullets that kept dropping among our ranks. With dawn on the 15th the several members of our body militant were at their posts, prepared for the work before them. As the 10th moved forward past a strip of dense jungle that skirts the river Tonse, a smart fire was opened upon us from the thicket, as also from a grove at some distance across that stream.

The first of these positions was at once attacked by our artillery, the infantry rapidly following; by means of a dilapidated

177

bridge hastily repaired, some cavalry and artillery got across and so attacked the second.

Other portions of our force were engaged with similar activity at the points assigned to them respectively, the result being, that after losing considerably in their numbers, the rebels fled pell-mell, and as we entered the city only some of their killed and wounded were anywhere met with. It was subsequently found that they had lost some guns, much equipage and stores, and that, under command of Koer Singh, they were in full flight towards the Ganges.

When, as already mentioned, the rebels from their position in the jungle opened fire upon the 10th, the demeanour of our men, hardened as they were by long service in India, and accustomed to the work of war, was such as vividly to illustrate the advantages of having old soldiers under such circumstances. Although taken by surprise, our men wavered not; with equanimity our colonel,[2] as he turned towards them, said, "Steady, men, steady." There was a sharp fire of musketry into the brushwood, instantly followed by a charge with the bayonet; native voices were heard as the *sepoys* recognised the soldiers they had to deal with, calling to their comrades, "*Bhago, bhago bhai, dus pultan aya*" (Run, brothers, run; the 10th have come). A minute more, and those who escaped bayonet thrusts by our men were in rapid flight.

Resulting from the day's encounter a considerable number of dead had to be interred, and wounded attended to. For the latter accommodation had to be procured, as well as for our sick, whose numbers had been rendered considerable by the great fatigue and exposure undergone during our recent long and arduous marches. As a guard to those so provided for, as well as to hold the city now in our power against further attack, and leave our force unencumbered for further action, the 34th was detailed to fulfil both duties.

A column under command of Brigadier Douglas started in pursuit of the body of rebels directly under Koer Singh. They

2. William Fenwick, than whom a more upright man could not be named.

178

having made a stand against Douglas as soon as the first panic of defeat had somewhat subsided, the pursuing column was on 17th reinforced by additional artillery, cavalry, and part of the 84th. Within a few hours thereafter the sound of active firing told us what was taking place; then the arrival of wounded men declared that serious work was being done. In due time we learned that the rebels had been defeated, a hundred of their number killed, and one of their guns captured.

Among the wounded so brought in was Mr. Venables, an indigo planter, a typical representative of the rough, ready, and energetic men who collectively become the makers of Greater Britain. Mr. Venables had, by his own force of character, prevented open revolt in the district of Azimghur after the 17th Native Infantry had mutinied, and, by means of levies raised and commanded by himself, repelled an attack by the latter; subsequently on various occasions he was in actual conflict against the rebels. Gangrene of the wounded shoulder took place, and within a very short time his death occurred, much to the sorrow and regret of those of us with whom he had been associated.

After his death it was discovered that he wore upon his bosom the wedding ring of his deceased wife. She had died at Azimghur, and now his body was laid in a grave close to the remains of her for whom his affection was manifest in tangible form.

On the 23rd General Lugard learned that notwithstanding their recent defeat the rebels under Koer Singh were advancing, as if to threaten Ghazepore. At 9 p.m. our force was in motion towards them. The night march was long and trying; for some hours our way was enlivened by the clear moonlight, but the air was hot and sultry. Occasional halts were necessary to enable the men to rest for a little, and refresh themselves with draughts of water.

Arrived at Mohumdee next morning, several hours elapsed before camp equipage arrived and tents were pitched, for as on various previous occasions our men outmarched their transport train. There news reached camp that Koer Singh had so far succeeded that nearly all the men commanded by him had got across the Ganges; but that Douglas, having arrived and opened fire upon them from the left bank, their chief had been severely wounded,[3] and of themselves many put *hors de combat*.

Later in the day the painful news circulated in camp that a small force, composed of men of 35th, the Naval Brigade, and some Sikhs, sent from Arrah to intercept the rebels then in rapid flight from the Ganges to Jugdispore, had met with disaster at their hands. The force referred to was that under the command of Captain Le Grand, 35th Regiment.

Two successive marches during the hottest period of each day, and we were at Ghazepore. Officers and men, forced by reason of seasonal temperature to dispense with outer uniform, wore only *khakee* trousers and woollen shirts, the sleeves turned up for sake of comfort. Thus equipped, dusty, and grimy, our aspect presented a sorry contrast to the neat and in some instances elegant turnout of men and women who rode out from cantonments to see our force march into camp.

Resuming the march next morning, the occurrence of a rain storm drenched us, but even that was an agreeable relief in the great heat and dust heretofore prevailing. No halt took place, but throughout that day and following night our wearied men continued what was indeed their forced march. By daylight on May 2 we arrived at Synhee Ghat. There, by means of steamers ready for the purpose, the work of crossing the Ganges rapidly proceeded, and by 9 a.m. we were in the Arrah district. We were now reunited to the column which under Douglas had been recently sent on from Azimghur, it having succeeded in preventing Koer Singh's men from falling upon Arrah after inflicting on a small body of our troops the disaster already mentioned.

Not until the 4th were all our stores and equipment transferred to the right side of the river, and our force in readiness for further work. The following morning our camp was pitched at Arrah,[4] and thus an opportunity afforded us to visit places in and

---

3. Of that wound Koer Singh soon thereafter died. The command of his forces then fell to Umeer Singh.

4. Here we received Government General Orders relating to the late Jounpore Field Force, my name in the list of those "mentioned."

around that station with which some recent painful events were associated. A building occupied a few months past by a civil servant now presented the appearance of a star-shaped fort from the embrasures of which the muzzles of guns projected; masses of ruins told where other bungalows had been. There stood the small fortified house, its walls loopholed and battered by rebel bullets, a memorial of the gallant defence made by Herwald Wake and his few comrades until relieved by Major Eyre.

At a little distance eastward from the city is the scene of the great disaster of July 30, already alluded to more than once; the road by which our men had marched, bordered on either side by isolated houses, at one spot by a clump of "toddy" palms, at another by a tope of mango trees; there the Hindoo temples at which, it was said, certain of our men on that occasion were offered as sacrifices to Kali; there the trees on which others were hung, though, as expressed by those on the spot, the events referred to are as far as possible "hushed up."

Information reached General Lugard that the rebels in considerable force had taken up a position at Jugdispore. He resolved to march upon and attack them without unnecessary delay. All extra establishment and equipment was left to be retained in store; sick and men otherwise non-effective eliminated; commissariat and transport suited for service on which we were about to enter, alone set apart for the purpose; mobility and efficiency the two qualities held in view.

In the lightest possible marching order our advance began on May 27. While it was yet dark, thirteen miles of road were got over; two more after daybreak, we then arrived at our intended camping ground; our only incident the capture of a spy,[5] in the act of counting the numbers and noting the composition of our column. The rebels had determined to oppose us *en route*. For that purpose they took up a position in a tract of jungle through which the road extended near Beheea; there our artillery opened fire upon them, and thence they were quickly expelled.

---

5. Captured by myself and duly handed over.
6. Comprising 10th Foot, Military Train Madras Artillery, Madras Rifles.

The aspect of the sky portended a dust storm; it was now upon us with all the usual violence of such meteors, the air so laden with dust that for a time all was dark. Then came a deluge of rain, soaking us completely, converting the hitherto parched ground into a swamp, but reducing the temperature from 100° to 85° As the sky became clear, a strong body of rebels were observed advancing towards us. At once a party was dispatched against them; brisk fire by the artillery, then our cavalry dashed in among them; they broke up and soon disappeared in the jungle. All through next night the camp was on the alert; pickets patrolled in all directions. In early morning of the 9th our advance was resumed.

During the march parties of rebels hovered on either flank, but at a safe distance from our column. As we neared the town of Jugdispore the enemy advanced upon us from front and flanks. When they came within striking distance, our column, already prepared for such an emergency, took the initiative; our men, to use their own expression, "went at them with a will." Before sunset that town, together with the palace of Koer Singh, were in our possession.

The 10th was a day of comparative quiet; men had to rest after their arduous work; those prostrated by heat and fatigue be attended to, information obtained .regarding movements of the fugitive enemy, and arrangements made for further action against them. While our force was thus enjoying comparative quiet, news reached our commander that the rebels had taken up a position at Chitowrah, situated deep in a dense jungle, some seven miles distant from our present camp; that a column comprising the 6th Regiment was in a position near Peroo to co-operate with us; that the column under Sir Hugh Rose was steadily closing around Jhansi; and that in Rohilcund our troops had obtained several important successes.

In the forenoon of the 11th a sufficient guard for its protection being left in camp, a strong body[6] of our force marched to attack the rebel position at Chitowrah. It had not proceeded more than three miles when an earthwork across the road for a short time interrupted progress; that obstacle overcome, a heavy fire from the dense jungle on our flanks and front opened upon us. As a reply our artillery opened with grape, after which skirmishers dashed into the thick forest, with the result that they carried all before them; but pursuit was impossible by reason of its density.

The heat of the day, great as it was in the open ground, was overpowering while we traversed the forest already mentioned. It was fortunate for all of us that this contingency had been foreseen and provided for by General Lugard; skins full of water, carried by elephants, camels, and bullocks, forming part of our equipment on the occasion. At short intervals of time and distance, soldiers and officers indiscriminately placed themselves under the open mouths of those skins, had their heads and clothing drenched; then continuing their march until the hot wind effected complete evaporation, they again and again underwent a similar ordeal. Nevertheless, many staggered, some fell from heat and exhaustion, others gasped for breath. Considerable numbers had to be brought along in *doolies*; among those so prostrated was Colonel Fenwick.[7] Exhausted as we were, it was fortunate for us that our enemies were wanting in resolution to take advantage of our condition.

Wearied and fatigued as were men and officers, little in the way of food was needed. Tea—that ever-agreeable beverage under such circumstances—was about the only thing obtainable at the time. Rest was out of the question during the night. Impressions of the day's work, repeated pings of musketry from the adjoining jungle, the thud of bullets on the ruined walls among which we lay, the occasional arrival of wounded men,—all combined to banish sleep; while to those engaged in looking after sick and wounded, whose numbers had become considerable, their work left them worn out and exhausted.

Daylight of the 12th revealed to us the scene of action. In jun-

---

7. An honourable man, considerate and straightforward in official as in private relations, he had effected much during the time he held command to restore to their normal state things already alluded to.

gle recesses mangled corpses; in the ruins, now utilised as "barracks" for effectives, and hospital for those struck down, whether by wounds or sickness, heavy moans of the suffering were intermingled with coarse jests of their more fortunate comrades.

The unpleasant fact transpired that our commissariat supplies had fallen into the hands of the rebels, while the force was engaged against them in the jungle as already mentioned. Breakfast for men and officers became a meal more nominal than real; orders were issued for the march to be resumed southward, so that our force might the more effectively co-operate with another making its way from that direction.

Early in the afternoon our force was on its march towards Peroo, with a view to effect that junction. As we advanced, the forest became less and less dense; emerging therefrom into open country, the burnt remains of huts and villages were passed. Some stray shots reached us from small concealed bodies of the enemy, but these were quickly silenced by parties of our men detached for that purpose. Without opposition in more serious form we arrived, while it was still daylight, at a mango tope, in which we bivouacked for the night, all necessary precautions being first taken against surprise. During that night a thunderstorm burst over us; this was followed by heavy downpour of rain, which soaked us to a degree that made sorry objects of us, situated as we then were, and at the same time reduced the ground that formed our beds to the condition of a marsh.

A raid was made upon cattle and rice, both of which were found among some ruined huts; the former were shot, and with the latter cooked, thus meal thus provided being savoury or otherwise according to whether individuals had or had not in their haversacks a small reserve of salt. At dawn next morning a strong party was detached to bring in supplies sent on to us from camp. It was not long before that escort was engaged with the rebels by whom it was attacked *en route,* and having defeated them, proceeded to obtain the needed supplies, with which in due time it returned to us.

As a part of that escort were some young soldiers of the 6th

Foot, recently arrived from the Cape of Good Hope. On their arrival back from that duty they were in so exhausted a condition that when time arrived to break up our bivouac they had to be removed by means of bullock-carts, elephants, and gun-carriages; the older soldiers of the same party, though much exhausted, were able to resume the march with their respective companies.

In the great heat now prevailing, the distance of nineteen miles that separated us from our standing camp was got over by ten o' clock that day; many so exhausted that, unable to keep up with the column, they followed as best they could, arriving as so many stragglers, but fortunately for them, unmolested and undiscovered by the rebels. During the absence of our column, our camp, left under protection of the 84th, was threatened by the rebels, who, however, were easily beaten off.

An attempt, made by men engaged for the purpose, to burn down the jungle—work in which had already cost us the lives of many men—was but partially successful. While at one point this was in' progress, from another came indications of attack by a considerable body of well-armed rebels. The 10th were quickly in movement towards them, a few of their bullets telling among our ranks. Soon, however, the enemy disappeared in the dense forest, our men returning to the comparative quiet and "comfort" of their tents.

Short was the rest enjoyed by them. On the third day an attack from our side was directed upon two villages occupied by the rebels in our near vicinity. Similar attacks on other villages succeeded each other; a convoy with supplies from our base at Arrah arrived; attempts on a larger scale than heretofore to burn down the forest were made, but unsuccessfully; and so, with the hot season upon us, did all concerned try their best to carry out the general work we had to do.

Some idea of the physical condition of our troops may best be gathered from the particulars now to be given. Soon after the middle of May fevers and bowel disorders had become very prevalent among them; in other ways they suffered severely from the prevailing heat and fatigue. As to myself, according to my diary, "from the time I became attacked at Azimghur, I have found it impossible to throw off my illness, and now am exhausted and debilitated to a great degree by the continued heat. Were it not my duty to hold out for the benefit of my wife and children, I would certainly apply for sick leave."

By that time, although our force had been only ten days in the field and jungle near Jugdispore, the number of non-effectives was so great as to seriously impair its efficiency and mobility; as many of these as could be so disposed of were accordingly sent under strong cavalry escort to Arrah. Cases of sunstroke were of occasional occurrence, though far less so than we had expected. Our transport suffered scarcely, if at all, in a less degree than our men, thus still further adding to the daily increasing difficulties under which we were expected to act as an efficient force. Another phase of our difficulties arose from the want of vegetables as part of our food. From the day when we first took the field supplies in this respect have been absent, the result being that men and officers are more or less suffering from land scurvy.

On the 20th our force made an attack on the village of Dhuleeppore, recently destroyed, but in the ruins of which a body of rebels had assembled. The result of that attack was discomfiture to them, though, unhappily, unusually heavy loss to the assailants.

Then followed a few days of comparative rest to our men; but meanwhile the rebels reoccupied the position from which so recently they had been driven. Arrangements were accordingly made for a renewed attack on that place.

At daylight on the 20th our force was in motion: one portion by a road just within the skirt of jungle, a second along the plain on which the affair of a few days before took place. As they drew close upon the rebel position, fire was opened from two howitzers captured on the occasion of the disaster to the party under Captain Le Grand already mentioned. Three rounds were fired before the 10th and 84th were able "to get at" the rebels.

Once among them, the guns were quickly recaptured, many of the gunners killed, the rebels in flight. Our men returned to their tents.

Our camp ground had become so offensive, and otherwise objectionable, that, leaving for a time a body of our force sufficiently strong to hold its own in case of emergency, the larger portion, under orders by General Lugard, proceeded to take up a fresh position. The move involved a march of four miles and upwards. While *en route* we traversed the scene of Le Grand's disaster. Isolated bones, some partly gnawed, lay scattered about; fragments of utensils of sorts strewed the surface,—sad relics, in their several ways, of the episode referred to. A halt was made; the fragments of what had been gallant men carefully collected and most reverently interred. We then resumed our way.

The numbers of sick and wounded had now exceeded the capacity of our transport; it became a matter of necessity to get rid of them, so that the force might be left ready prepared for further action. Being provided with a strong cavalry escort, I started with a full convoy of such non-effectives. We traversed a piece of country directly in front of the rebels, halting under the shelter of a mango tope during the hottest hours of daylight; resumed the journey at nightfall, and reached Arrah before daybreak. There the sick and wounded were disposed of in hospital; our return journey quickly resumed, and without adventure we were again with our force in time for further work.

A few days prior to the date now reached, a messenger had been sent with dispatches from General Lugard to the officer in command of a column co-operating with his own. The man presented a sorry plight as he returned to camp; his nose cut off, his right hand severed at the wrist, his face and other parts of his person besmeared with blood, himself faint, bewildered, and dazed. After a time he related the story of his capture. He had reached his destination without mishap, had delivered the dispatches of which he was bearer, received those in reply, and started on his return journey with them.

While passing through a rebel village on his way he was arrested, his papers taken from him, he himself ordered for execution, as traitor and spy. On the plea that in the state of mutilation inflicted upon him his appearance would be more deterrent among possible waverers in the rebel cause than would be the fact of his being put to death, the extreme penalty was commuted.

A body of rebels having destroyed an indigo factory and taken up a position at Kishwa, our force started at 3 a.m. on the 2nd of June towards that point. As we approached it, a heavy though happily ineffectual fire was opened against our ranks. The 10th marched steadily onwards. The rebels did not long remain to permit our men to close with them; pell-mell they fled, the Madras guns sending several charges of grape-shot after them, the cavalry then taking up the pursuit We afterwards bivouacked in the open.

Driven thence, the rebels returned to their former position at Chitowrah. By daylight on the 4th of June our force advanced upon them in two separate columns: the one along the narrow jungle road already mentioned; the other, under the command of Brigadier Douglas, by the southern border of the same jungle. As we neared the densest part of forest, in the heart of which lay that hunting seat of Koer Singh, we suddenly found ourselves exposed in a semi-circle of fire in front and both our flanks; fortunately without much damage to our numbers.

There was a momentary halt, then a cheer, and into the forest dashed the 10th, trusting to their bayonets rather than their rifle fire. The rebels fled, at first through and from the thicket whence their attack had been made, our men following close upon them; next, through ruins of houses and enclosures; through a cactus hedge, across an open plain, our soldiers gaining upon them in the race, the result being a loss to our enemies of ninety-four, fallen by bayonet thrust of our regiment alone. Wearied and exhausted, a short rest had to be allowed to men and officers.

In our return journey towards camp we again traversed the ground over which the running fight described had taken place; the rebels killed in the early part of the day were represented by so many masses of skeletons, blood covered, some few shreds of flesh still adhering, thus telling what had been the work done in the interval by jackals, dogs, and vultures.

The immediate result of the rebel defeat at Chitowrah was that their force divided itself into small parties, each of which seemed to proceed on its own initiative, some as marauders, others with the apparent object of making for Buxar, and thence across the Ganges. With a view to act against the latter, a portion of our force, reduced as it now was by casualties and sickness, was placed under command of Brigadier Douglas, and proceeded on the duty assigned to it.

To the regret of all associated with him, General Lugard completely broke down in health; several of the officers were ill or had been invalided; the numbers of our soldiers who had become non-effective was very large. Under the circumstances in which we were thus placed, the fact became evident that unless it was intended by the responsible authorities that our force should be permitted to melt away and so cease to exist, a speedy return to cantonments was necessary to preserve that portion which still existed of its component elements.

Great, therefore, was the relief with which, in obedience to orders to return to cantonments, we marched away from Jugdispore on June 15. Our first day's march was no more than six miles long. Our men, however, had no longer the stimulus of expected fight to brace them up; many fell out *en route,* to come in as stragglers during the day. Continuing our journey, we once again passed through Arrah, then crossed the Soane, marching into quarters at Dinapore on the 19th of that month. The Azimghur Field Force had done the work assigned to it, and now ceased to exist as such.

The arrival of General Orders,[8] in which were contained the official dispatches relating to work performed by the force of which we had so recently formed a part, became naturally enough an event of importance to most of us, gratification to some, disappointment to others. Much praise was accorded to the 10th Regiment, as a whole, for arduous work efficiently done, and special reference made to individual officers whose services

8. Government General Orders, dated Allahabad, June 16, 1858.

were "mentioned" in those dispatches. Paragraph 19 of the Orders in question gave the report by Sir Edward Lugard thus:

> I beg most especially to recommend to His Excellency's notice —— [myself], Surgeon of the 10th Foot and Senior Medical Officer in charge of this force; his exertions have been untiring; though at times suffering from sickness, he never quitted his post, but continued his valuable superintendence. I feel more indebted to him than I can express.

With reference to which the entry made in my diary at the time was:

> I am thankful to God for having enabled me to fulfil my duties satisfactorily, and, for the sake of my dear wife and children, hope advancement may speedily follow so handsome an acknowledgment of services performed.

A few days afterwards we had the further gratification of reading "Orders" awarding to each of us six months' *batta*.

CHAPTER 17

1858-1859. Dinapore—Plymouth

A period of rest in cantonments had become a matter of necessity to restore physical efficiency to our regiment, worn out as men and officers were by service in the field. The ordinary duties incidental to barrack existence in India were performed by all, our spare time devoted to current records of events announced from day to day by the newspapers. A few examples now follow.

No sooner had our force departed from Jugdispore than the rebels returned to their former positions in the extensive jungle by which that place is surrounded. Among the proceedings taking place elsewhere was the defeat, by Sir Hope Grant, of a strong rebel force at Nawabgunge. In the vicinity of Shahjehanpore, the Moulvie already mention was killed by the troops of a Rajah[1] who had risen against his authority. Gwalior had been recaptured; the Ranee of Jhansi killed while leading her troops at that place against the Central India Force. Reports of disaffection in certain Bombay regiments.

In our own near neighbourhood, a threatened outbreak by the prisoners in Patna gaol led to the dispatch thither of two companies of the 10th. The rebels had collected in a body of considerable strength at Chuprah, from which position they were committing depredations on trading boats on the Gan-

---

1. Namely, Juggernath Singh, Rajah of Powayne, a man who, in the early days of the mutiny, had acted in a very unfeeling manner towards such fugitives as fell into his hands.

ges; a portion of the 35th was accordingly dispatched against them. Another party of rebels threatening Bulliah, a detachment of the 10th proceeded by steamer towards that place. Various lines of communication were kept open by parties of troops placed at suitable points along them. The position at Arrah was so strengthened as to be secure against attack. The arrival of a small kind of gunboat intended for use on rivers was in its way important, as indicating the introduction of a new means of attack.

At this time the issue of certain Proclamations by Government seemed to attract much attention among the rebels still in the field; the tenor of the one an invitation to them to lay down their arms, the other in effect confiscating the property of landowners in Oude, with a few exceptions. "It is all very well," said they, "to invite us to come in, lay down our arms, and accept forgiveness; but why make the offer if you have the power to subdue us?"

"Hitherto, if we committed murder, robbery, or burnt houses, we were hanged, imprisoned, or put on the roads for life; now we have done all these things, and we are invited to accept forgiveness. Truly this is a great raj; may it live forever!"

Adverting to the first of those Proclamations, Lord Canning had expressed himself:

It is impossible that the justice, charity, and kindliness, as well as the true wisdom which mark these words, should not be appreciated.

That is the way they were so. The second was at once called "the Confiscation Proclamation"; its almost immediate effect, an outbreak of hostility among chiefs who were otherwise more or less ready to remain passive if not actually favourable to existing law. At a subsequent date it was cancelled.

The debates in Parliament on these dispatches and many other comments on them were daily perused with great interest, not only by ourselves, but, as we learnt, by the rebels still in arms, the several views expressed by them somehow reaching cantonments.

The publication of orders, in which it was considered that services performed by the Sikhs were referred to in exaggerated terms' as compared with the purely British, produced for the time being one effect to which allusion may here be made.

"Why," said a very intelligent officer of that nationality, who was well known to most of us in cantonments, "you admit yourselves that we saved India for you; if we can do that for you foreigners, why should we not take the country for ourselves?"

At the very time he spoke there were 82,000 Sikh troops in British employ. It was therefore not altogether subject of surprise to learn, as we did, that a mutinous plot had been discovered in the 10th Sikh Infantry at the distant station of Dhera Ishmail Khan.

Nor were matters satisfactory on the part of the Ghoorkhas, recently our "allies." The circumstance transpired that correspondence had been discovered between some of the higher authorities of Nepaul and the Royal family of Oude; that Jung Bahadur had expressed himself dissatisfied with degree of acknowledgment awarded by the Indian Government for services rendered by himself and by his troops.

With the advance of the rainy season sickness and death made sad havoc among our ranks. Meanwhile a state of unrest among the general population became more and more apparent, fanned as it was by reports circulated among them that large reinforcements from England would speedily arrive. Nor was that unrest confined to the non-military sections; some of the remaining *sepoys* believed to be "staunch" were said to have been detected in treasonable correspondence with their brethren in open rebellion; that representatives of mutineers had taken service in the ranks of the police force.

The 1st of November, 1858, began an era memorable in the history of India. On that day was read at every military station throughout the country the Proclamation by the Queen, declaring the transference to Her Majesty of the governing power hitherto exercised by the Honourable East India Company, the

10th Regiment and other troops occupying our present station being paraded at the civil station of Bankipore to impart additional splendour to an otherwise imposing ceremony. The Proclamation was read by the Commissioner of the district, an immense concourse of natives being present on the occasion.

With reference to the portions of that Proclamation in which, under certain specified conditions, pardon and amnesty are offered to rebels, the *Punjabee* newspaper of October 30 publishes a return of the army still opposed to us in Oude alone, comprising, according to figures there given, 79 chiefs, with an aggregate of 271 guns, 11,660 cavalry, 242,100 infantry, or 253,760 men in all; an imposing force indeed, considering that the suppression of the outbreak is declared to have been accomplished.

From the rebels still in the field, various comments on the terms so offered reached our cantonments. They considered that for crimes committed the *sepoys* deserved punishment by death, nor could they understand the exemption to that penalty now expressed.

> "As an earthquake"—according to their "prophets"—"has three waves, so will there be three shocks to British power in India: one we have just had; a second will occur a few years hence; the last after a longer interval, when the British position in India will vanish."

The arrival of papers with a new warrant [9] for the Medical Department of the Army naturally enough was of considerable interest to those of us who belonged to that branch of the military service. As expressed in my diary at the time:

> Most liberal it is, wiping away at one swoop the grievances under which the Department has laboured, and making it, as it ought to be, one of the best, if not the very best, in the Army.

The great importance of the duties pertaining to that department in relation to individual needs and general military effi-

---

9. Of October 1, 1858.

ciency of a force was then prominently in my view from actual experience.

Shortly after the Proclamation by Her Majesty was read, a counter document of similar nature was issued by the Begum of Lucknow; but the latter produced little if any effect upon the rebels or their chiefs, numbers of both "coming in "one after another to make their submission. An attempt was made by a leading journal[10] to ascertain the number of persons who, being convicted of crimes against the State, had suffered the penalty of death. They were, according to that paper, as follows, from the outbreak of the Mutiny, namely:—

By military tribunal, executed by hanging, 86; by civil tribunal, 300; the number shot by musketry, 628; blown from guns, 1,370; making a total of 2,384.

The deposed King of Delhi recently passed our station by steamer, *en route* to Calcutta, and finally to Rangoon, there to spend the remaining portion of his life. The event gave rise to comment in respect to the action of the old king against the Indian Government, including his correspondence with the Shah of Persia in 1856; his reputed sanction of atrocities at Delhi in May, '57; his correspondence with Lucknow, etc. Another subject of talk was the reported escape of the Nana, the truth of which was soon thereafter confirmed. Lastly, the publication of correspondence between Colonel Edwards, Sir John Lawrence, and the Viceroy,[11] in respect to that portion of the Proclamation which related to native customs, religious and otherwise, afforded ample subject to discuss in our social coteries.

In the early days of 1859 came the welcome orders that all detached parties of the 10th should rejoin Headquarters, for the purpose of volunteering preparatory to the departure of the regiment for England. Other orders directed various reductions to be made in military establishments now in India; among them the withdrawal of several time-expired regiments, and the

10. *Friend of India,* December 2, 1858.
11. Afterwards noticed in Chambers' *History of the Revolt,* page 607.

return to their respective ships of the Naval Brigades temporarily employed; that regiments still in the field should proceed to quarters; brigadiers commanding columns cease to hold appointments as such—thus declaring in effect that the campaign connected with the great Mutiny was ended. But the facts were well known that bodies of rebels and mutineers were in the field, special forces actually employed against them; that bodies of disaffected had taken refuge in Nepaul. These and various other incidents were looked upon as so many supplements to the great drama at the end of which official orders declared that we had arrived.

Now there occurred an event the outcome of which to several men who, like myself, had held distinct charges of troops on active service, was much chagrin and disappointment; namely, our supersession in promotion by four officers, personally good, but who, though in the Crimea, had neither there nor elsewhere held equivalent positions. Some little time thereafter there appeared in a service journal[12] a leading article "On the partiality and injustice to the Department exhibited in the late promotions." This was the first outcome of a warrant regarding which first impressions were as already recorded.

At last came orders for the 10th to prepare for an early march towards the port of embarkation for England, and that meantime volunteering should be open to soldiers desiring to prolong their service in India. All such orders were obeyed with the greatest possible alacrity. The usual formalities on similar occasions being attended to, 141 of our men availed themselves of the option thus given them, and so ceased to belong to the corps in which they had performed much excellent work under very trying circumstances.

On an intervening Sunday a farewell sermon[13] was preached to the regiment in our garrison church, and as I noted at the time, "strange as it seems, some of the soldiers were visibly af-

---

12. *Naval and Military Gazette,* January 8, 1859.
13. Colossians 3. 15: *And let the peace of God rule in your hearts, to the which also ye are called in one body; and be ye thankful.*

fected thereby"; but as I have had numerous opportunities of seeing, soldiers of the period now referred to, notwithstanding the undoubted roughness of the great majority, had in their numbers many men keenly sensitive to the finer impulses of our common human nature.

Before daylight on February 10, our regiment began its march, "played out" of Dinapore by the band of the 19th Foot. Eight days thereafter we encamped in near vicinity of Gyah, a place sacred to Buddhists, and interesting in other ways. Two days more and we were on the Grand Trunk Road. Soon at the hot wells of Burkutta, the water of which, clear and having a slight odour of sulphur, is said to have many medicinal virtues.

In observing the necessary custom on a march, of halting on the seventh day, an opportunity was afforded those of us interested in such matters, to ascend the hill of Parisnath. Occupying the eastern tableland of the Vindyha range, itself 4,449 feet in height, like Mount Aboo on the west of the same range, its summit is covered with small Jain temples. Its sides are clothed with dense forests of sal (*Vateria indica*).

In the course of our march, several trains of camels or *kafilats*, with their Cabulee drivers, were met, as they were on their return journey from Calcutta to Affghanistan. In accordance with the custom of the time, they had begun their journey from Cabul eight months previous, and hoped to return at the end of four more, thus completing it in one year. These *kafilats* brought with them for sale in India, and Calcutta more especially, fruit of different kinds, spices, skins, *asafœtida*, and *salep*;[14] with the proceeds of the sale of which they purchased and carried back with them bales of cotton goods, and others of European manufacture.

These caravans, including camels, drivers, and "followers," presented a picturesque and patriarchal scene, as in long lines they seemed to glide along the road. Arrived at Raneegunge, our camp was pitched for the last time. There a delay of several days took place, while arrangements were in progress for embarka-

---

14. Root of *Orchis mascula*.

tion; hurried journeys by rail to and from Calcutta being made by those of us whose duty it was to carry those arrangements into effect. A series of coal-mines situated not far from our camp were being worked; but the industry was, comparatively speaking, in its infancy.

In the early morning of St. Patrick's Day, the regiment, stepping out cheerfully to the familiar music appropriate to the occasion, and dear to Irish soldiers, marched away from camp to railway station; thence proceeded by train to Howrah, then by river steamer to the ship *King Philip,* and so embarked. On the second day thereafter our ship, taken in tow by a river tug, began her homeward voyage. As we glided past Fort William, a Royal salute, fired from its ramparts, was a gratifying compliment paid by order of Government to the departing regiment for services performed by it during a most eventful episode in India's history. Wearied and worn out as our men were as a result of those services, no cheer was raised in response to the unusual compliment being paid to them.

The order by Government, so alluded to was in these terms:—

The Calcutta Gazette Extraordinary, Friday, March 18, 1859. No. 360 of 1859. Notification. Fort William, Military Department. The 18th March, 1859.—Her Majesty's 10th Regiment of Foot is about to embark for England. His Excellency the Governor-General cannot allow this regiment to pass through Calcutta without thanking the officers and men for all the good service which they have rendered in the last two eventful years: first, in the outbreaks at Benares and Dinapore; next, as a part of the Column under their former Commander, Brigadier-General Franks; and more lately in the harassing operations conducted by Brigadier-General Sir E. Lugard and Brigadier Douglas on either bank of the Ganges. The Governor-General in Council desires, in taking leave of the 10th Regiment, to place on record his cordial appreciation of their valuable services. The regiment will be saluted by the guns of Fort William on leaving Calcutta. By order of his Excellency the Viceroy and Governor-General of India in Council.—R.J.H. Birch, Major-General, Secretary to the Government of India.

[Subsequently the officers of the 10th, including myself, received among us nine promotions and honorary distinctions for the services above alluded to.]

During the homeward voyage several deaths occurred among our men, exhausted as so many of them were by fatigue and exposure on service. Perhaps it was that the incidents of that service had to some extent affected the feelings heretofore so often manifested by soldiers in presence of death among their comrades; at any rate, it became a source of regret to some of our numbers to observe now the indifference shown on such occasions; indeed, scarcely was the solemnity of committing a body to the deep finished than games, songs, music, or dancing were resumed by parties of the men. The long rest afforded by the voyage did much to restore health to men and officers, and in other ways was beneficial to us all.

As we neared England a pilot boarded our ship. He had with him a bundle of papers, from which we learned, among other matters, of the occurrence of war in the Quadrilateral, full details being given of the great battles of Magenta and Solferino. In the accounts contained in the same papers of the state of public affairs preceding that campaign, a probable explanation was afforded of the suddenness with which active measures against the mutineers had ceased, and considerable forces withdrawn from India.

At Gravesend, on July 13, the regiment transhipped to the *Himalayah,* and so was conveyed to Plymouth, there to be quartered in the Citadel. A few days thereafter,[15] I had the happiness of being with my beloved wife and children, grateful in spirit to Providence that life was preserved through the arduous ordeal now relegated to the past.

---

15. July 24.

CHAPTER 18

1859-1860. Plymouth—Devonport

Soon after our arrival I became the possessor of a horse and carriage, both purchased from "a friend." With pleasant anticipations I started on our first drive, accompanied by my wife and her lady friend. We had not proceeded far along the country road before the animal bolted clean away; after wildly rushing for some considerable distance, the carriage came in contact with the embankment, was upset and broken to pieces, the two ladies severely injured. The accident happened at the entrance to a country house; the ladies were admitted thereto for a little, a glass of wine given to each; they were driven home, after which no inquiry was made regarding them.

This first experience of "hospitality" impressed us at the time, and now is noted as in its way characteristic. We had not been "introduced" to the family.

Unfortunately it so happened that among the men of the 10th there were some who used not wisely the balance of "*batta*" still remaining unspent by them. The result was that they brought obloquy upon themselves, and to some extent upon their more steady and well-behaved comrades who were altogether undeserving of it. So it happens on other occasions; the actual number of men in a regiment who commit crimes may be small, though their offences may be statistically considerable.[1]

1. The 10th Regiment was composed of the following, according to religious denomination; namely, Episcopalians, 29 officers and 236 men; Presbyterians, 8 and 28; Roman Catholics, 5 and 301. It may be taken as an example of an "English" regiment.

In September attention was painfully drawn to the unfortunate failure at Taku of the war vessels conveying the British and French ambassadors to the Peiho *en route* to Pekin, that failure involving the loss of three gunboats and 464 men belonging to them. From that moment it became evident that troops and ships must prepare for service in the Far East, and although, as the 10th had so recently landed, it was unlikely that the regiment would as a whole be concerned, it was probable . that some individual officers might be so; several of us accordingly took an opportunity of making ourselves acquainted with the current of events in China from the date of the *Arrow* affair in October, 1856, to that of the Taku incident alluded to.

Following close upon the news of that disaster came the wreck of the *Royal Charter,* involving the loss of 470 lives, near Bangor, during one of those autumn storms so frequent on English coasts. Public sympathy was much aroused by these events, quickly following each other as they did. Unhappily the last named was not at the time isolated of its kind, though in its details not exceeded in painful accompaniments by any.

A new war vessel—the *Narcissus* frigate of fifty guns—being to be launched, the ceremony proved not only interesting but impressive, in respect to sentiments it evolved. An immense assembly met by invitation in Devonport Dockyard to witness the event; as the hour of four struck, the beautiful ship glided amidst a round of cheers into what thenceforward was to be her proper element; her career in the future in that respect like the career of the new-born infant—uncertain, beset by risks.

Very different in character was another "function" at which I "assisted"; namely, a lecture with demonstrations on phrenology, the "correctness" of that "science" being illustrated by the lecturer by references to the characteristics of the Hindoo in respect to mildness, gentleness, and tractability. To those of us recently returned from scenes already described, his remarks and demonstrations seemed outcomes of misapplied knowledge. Yet, such as they were, they "went down" with the enlightened British public, as represented by that particular audience.

Various circumstances, domestic and foreign, combined to render regimental life one of uncertainty, at the particular time now referred to. In India more than one column of our forces were actively engaged against the rebels who declined the terms of the gracious. Proclamation already mentioned. The recently enlisted men for so-called "European" regiments of the late East India Company had combined in what was called "The White Mutiny"; they were shipped to England, there to be discharged the service.[2] Disaffection had appeared in two native cavalry regiments stationed at Hyderabad.[3]

With regard to Europe, the condition of affairs in and relating to Italy was disturbed and uncertain. In France, the effusions of certain colonels, added to other indications hostile to England, seemed to have an unpleasant significance, more especially that in which an appeal was made to the Emperor "to give the word, and the infamous haunt in which machinations so infernal are planned"—namely, London—"should be destroyed forever."

A strong fleet of combined English and French warships proceeded to China. Extensive stores and supplies of all kinds were shipped for that destination, magazines were replenished; appearances indicated that important operations were in the near future. Uncertainty and speculation regarding probable events pervaded all ranks pertaining to regiments now available for emergent service; all held themselves prepared accordingly.

Various Militia regiments, embodied during the Crimean War, still occupied barracks throughout England; at Devonport and Plymouth the Warwickshire and Dublin Regiments, together with the Forfar Militia Artillery, being quartered. Second battalions were in progress of being added to the twenty-five first of the line. Now also, for the first time since the Revolutionary War, regiments of Volunteers were being rapidly formed. So important was the occasion considered to be that special invita-

---

2. Of their number a few enlisted into the 10th, and soon attempted to disseminate their particular doctrines. But Barrack-room Courts-Martial and sharp punishments—by means of belts—quickly convinced them that they were—so much matter in the wrong place.
3. 5th and 6th Madras.

tions were issued to witness in the Town Hall the first parade of the Volunteers belonging to what were called "The Three Towns," and to inaugurate the formation of the regiment so constituted. The building was well filled by officials and others; great was the enthusiasm with which the ceremony passed off, the numbers of Volunteers in the ranks of the new regiment being ninety-three.

Some changes, having for their object the improved condition of the soldier, were now in course of introduction. Thus orders were issued on the subject of corporal punishment, the infliction of which was reduced to a minimum. In other respects the stringent methods heretofore considered necessary for the maintenance of discipline were so relaxed that old officers were wont to predict a number of evil consequences as sooner or later sure to follow.

With the introduction of the national system of education into regimental schools, the reading of the Holy Bible in them was looked upon as seriously menaced in the present and threatened with prohibition in the near future. According to orders issued on the subject, "the Bible is only to be read, and religious instruction of any kind given, during one hour per week, and then in the presence of the Roman Catholic priest." Many among us looked with dread and apprehension to the probable outcome of the changes so begun.

That in the large garrison of Plymouth and Devonport there existed no regular hospital for the wives and children of soldiers seemed to most of us a very anomalous circumstance. Correspondence on the subject between myself and the Divisional authorities was without practical result. Taking advantage of the popularity and influence of Miss Nightingale at the War Office, I addressed myself to that lady. In a marvellously short space of time orders were received to set on foot such an establishment; they were quickly carried out, very much to the benefit of the classes for whom it was intended.

On January 15, 1860, I received a letter from the Registrar of the Bath, directing me to hold myself in readiness to proceed to Windsor, there to receive the Insignia of that Order, to which I had some months previously been gazetted.[4] Two days thereafter—namely,. on the 17th—a further letter ordering my attendance at Windsor Castle, at quarter before 3 p.m. precisely, on the 19th.

On the 18th I proceeded, taking my dear wife with me, to that Royal burgh. The early part of the forenoon of the 19th was occupied in visiting some of the points of interest connected with the castle, more especially the Round Tower and St. George's Chapel, the latter containing that most beautiful work of art, the cenotaph to the Princess Charlotte.

Punctually at the hour appointed, those of us who were to be similarly honoured drove to the Castle. We were shown into the Oak Room, and there, taking count of each other, discovered that our party numbered fourteen. Luncheon over, a messenger announced that Her Majesty was ready to begin the ceremony of investiture. The Lancaster Herald,[5] who had meantime very courteously initiated some of us in the formalities to be observed, then mustered us in our order. He led the way, we following, into the great corridor, at a door opening into which we were halted, to be called in our turn to the Royal presence.

The first to enter was an officer upon whom the honour of knighthood was to be conferred. Each Companion was summoned in his order of seniority as such. The cross with which we were severally to be invested was by the Lancashire Herald carried upon a cushion of crimson velvet. The door being opened, we separately entered a small apartment, at the further end of which stood the Queen; at her right side the Prince Consort. Our names announced, we advanced, making obeisance as we did so, knelt upon the right knee; the cross was attached over to the left breast by Her Majesty; we kissed hands, retired backwards, profoundly bowing the while. Thus we emerged, and the ceremony was over.[6]

---

4. *London Gazette,* May 14, 1859.

5. Mr. (afterwards Sir Albert) Woods.

6. I was the first regimental surgeon invested by Her Majesty with the Cross of the Bath.

Preparations on a large scale for the expedition to China were in rapid progress, the military forces to be sent thither comprising regiments direct from England, others, British and native, from India. Public attention and a good deal of adverse criticism were directed to what was looked upon as excessive naval and military estimates in a so-called time of profound peace. At important military and naval stations, fortifications were much extended, and newly armed with Armstrong guns; for, although there was much of what was ludicrous in the "boastings of the French Colonels," the fact was apparent that their expressions were not altogether unnoticed by our authorities.

Excursions in various directions were taken; some with the object of seeing places of historical interest, some to take note of the early spring flora, others to examine geological features of the neighbouring country. One such visit was to copper mines near Liskeard, there to see for the first time the beautiful "peacock" ore brought from the depths of earth and displayed to our gaze by means of a hammer wielded by the sturdy arms of "Captain Jane,"—for the superintendent of the mine was a woman so named.

At a little distance from the Canadian and Phœnix mines rises the Cheesewring, a granite hill some 1,200 feet in height, the rocks on its summit so piled upon each other as to thus give rise to its particular name. On some of those rocks were marks of boulder action, also tracings that bore distinct resemblance of vessels in ordinary use by Hindoos at their worship on the banks of the Hooghly, and now attributed to the Druids, one of whose places of sacrifice this *tor* may perhaps have been.

More and more did the state of uncertainty and unrest in which regimental officers had to perform their duties increase during the early months of the year, by the condition of affairs in Continental Europe. With regard to items of the general complication then noted, the following extract from my diary, written at the time, reads somewhat strangely today, namely:

"France resolved upon the annexation of Savoy, notwithstanding the strongly expressed opposition of England against that measure; the threatened occupation of Tetuan by Spain, opposed by England, as being against the terms on which England remained neutral between that country and Morocco."

The first decade of wedded life completed,[7] the following reference to the occasion was written at the time:

> Notwithstanding all that I have undergone since that event, sufficient of my early romance remains to enter in this place the motto which on that occasion surrounded the bon-bon broken by my bride and myself at our wedding luncheon—'My hopes are in the bud; bid them bloom.'

As the paragraph is being transcribed, the fifth decade is not far from completion. With affection chastened and sanctified by trial and affliction, I express to the Almighty humble gratitude that from bud my hopes have indeed advanced to bloom—holy and refined.

Towards the end of April, soldiers and officers of the 10th received their medals awarded for the campaign connected with the Indian Mutiny. No pomp and circumstance of military display took place on the occasion of their doing so. On the contrary, from the manner in which the distribution took place, all such accompaniments were intentionally avoided. It was while walking on the public thoroughfare in Devonport, that by accident, as it were, I met a sergeant in whose hand was a packet of little card-case boxes; one of these he presented to me—it contained my medal. I then continued on my way!

---

7. March 14.